Subjective atlas of Brussels

Subjective atlas of Brussels

Edited by
Annelys de Vet

CONTENTS

Proposition

To start with, I immediately regret writing in English. Brussels is about a lot of things, and certainly about the many different languages, cultures and backgrounds. It's the capital of diverse entities and can't be captured as a singularity, nor in a single image. Nevertheless, the representation of Brussels has recently become rather uniform. The terrorist attacks, the political turmoil and the throngs of journalists in Molenbeek pushed the narrative of the city far away from its reality on the ground.

Having lived in Brussels for more than 10 years now and having fallen in love with this undefinable metropolis, I keep being surprised by people I meet elsewhere in Belgium who have rarely travelled to Brussels or who consider it a dangerous place to live in. I wonder whether it has to do with the fact that it's often outsiders who speak about Brussels, or whether it's the savage dynamics of mass media, contiguously highlighting the exception, magnifying problems and capturing the temporality. Or is it the lack of diversity in the representative bodies, whether the city council or cultural institutes? The profound involvement of the residents in the development of the city and their experience of living here are aspects that remain underexposed in the media spectacle.

In this *Subjective Atlas*, more than 80 creative individuals visualized their view. What does it mean to be or to live in Brussels? What are the urgencies of the citizens? What are the particular qualities? Based on their own personal experiences and observations, they mapped out what makes life worth living here. From quay views [page 44] to high-rise-perspectives [page 48], from alternative playgrounds [page 108] to the last rays of sunshine [page 100] and from damaged bollards [page 60] to places of hope [page 124]. Over the course of several workshops and many encounters, the contributors captured their engagement in maps, inventories and drawings. Each work stems from involvement with the subjects and takes an engaged, critical and transparent position, not a neutral or so-called objective one. As such, the contributions not only show their own story, but also develop meta-reflections on contemporary forms of living together and community building.

This creative trajectory illustrates how design can be an important tool for soft power and how it helps to imagine a different future. The *Subjective Atlas* is therefore also a proposition for a creative mentality that is politically engaged, socially sensitive, collaborative in nature and transdisciplinary in its method.

Overall the book offers a platform for a bottom-up polyphonic visual dialogue about Brussels at this moment of time. I hope it can contribute to a better representation and understanding of a city with enormous potential. It's not an easy reality, nor a simple love. But one that is intense and enriching and one that can be life-changing. Brussels has taught me more about the world than any other city. It's a society that we can never capture, never fully understand or control. But it challenges us to find new languages to speak about who we are and what binds us.

I deeply want to thank all artists, designers, architects and creative minds who have generously contributed to this *Subjective Atlas* – taking pictures in the middle of the night, travelling to each commune, crossing borders, measuring distances and stretching their perspectives. It's through their accumulative voices that this Atlas wants to reclaim agency to the city's narrative.

If the city was a body part

On a beautiful summer night in June when the city was filled with carefree bliss and youthful candour, I gathered with friends at one of my favourite bars in the city centre, *Au Daringman*. After the usual catching up and playful banter, I rather haphazardly presented them with an unusual question: if the city was a body part, what would it be? After initial hesitation and bewilderment at the quirky nature of the enquiry, most of them delved into an enthusiastic reflection. They all agreed that it was definitely not the head, "because this city makes no sense at all". Indeed, when you live in Brussels you are constantly baffled by its unnecessarily complex nature: the city of only 1.2 million people is divided into 19 separate communes that each have their own mayor, administration and local council. Often this labyrinthine structure leads to absurd and infuriating situations, such as huge discrepancies in taxes between different boroughs or people with a resident's parking permit not being able to park across the street from their house because that street is part of another commune.

Marjorie Vandriessche page 52 and Gilberte Debeer page 50 capture these Kafkaesque scenarios in their works as, each in their own way, they make palpable the invisible borders that separate different parts of the city. The geographic division between the centre and the rest of the city, between underserved communities in the north and the leafy suburbs in the south and east, and the communes on either side of the canal continues to shape and segregate the city. The place I call home, for instance, Saint-Josse-ten-Noode, is known as the smallest, poorest, most densely populated commune. It is situated just a few blocks away from the impressive steel and glass buildings of the European Quarter. Brussels is made up of such heterogeneous micro-societies that live next to each other. Whenever I tell people from the southern part where I live, they first look at me as if I lived in a hostile, depraved, faraway region, before presenting me with a barrage of questions such as: "Do you feel at ease there? Do you feel safe walking alone at night? Isn't your neighbourhood really dirty?" Questions you would expect from someone who grew up in a small town in Flanders but not from a fellow Brusseleir. In our capital, however, your wanderings and social status are determined by the communal frontiers and physical layout of the city. The different alternative maps in the atlas – from Amina Saâdi's *The challenge* page 12 and Adrien Requin *A network among the inhabitants* page 14 to Sophie Bruyr's *Network* page 15 – all lay bare the palimpsestic nature of geographies, uncovering the meanings, connections and worlds that are hidden beneath the cartography of Brussels.

To return to the café conversation. After losing our train of thought during the third round of beers, one of my friends got back on topic and randomly shouted: "Brussels is the heart", followed by a dramatic silence. "Because", he resumed, "it's the heart of Belgium, and the heart of Europe". Even as he said it, his hesitant tone revealed that he was not entirely convinced by his own statement. Certainly, Brussels is at the centre of the country and the European Union as the (bilingual) capital of Belgium, of the Flemish Region and of the French-speaking Community, and as the unofficial capital of Europe. As a matter of fact, in an effort to establish a stronger brand identity, the Brussels-Capital Region recently incorporated a heart in its official logo and flag. And still, no one around the table seemed entirely persuaded. If anything, in Flanders, people seem to have fallen out of love with their national capital and feel little loyalty towards it. When I'm surrounded by people who live in Antwerp, Ghent or Leuven, I often find myself defending my newly adopted hometown from the one-dimensional depictions of Brussels as a dangerous hub of terrorists and a barely functioning political nightmare.

Just when we started to elaborate on the many stereotypes people associate with Brussels, our heated conversation was suddenly interrupted by a young man asking us for some change. He looked exceptionally fashionable with his striped t-shirt tucked into his ripped jeans and a pair of white Nike trainers on his feet. As we dropped the pennies in his open palm, a broad grin split his weather-beaten face and revealed some missing teeth. After he left, our conversation meandered back to the topic of the evening: "I think Brussels is like the intestines", someone said. As we burst out laughing, the person who had made the remark urged us to hear her out.

She argued that the reason why she chose this particular organ was because the city was so hard to digest – put differently: difficult to wrap your head around. Frankly, it is impossible to fully decipher the inner workings of Brussels. The city is an enigma, presenting itself daily in a multitude of ways. Well, if your city mascot is a little boy peeing, you are bound to be a peculiar, surprising place. Still, no one was willing to settle for the intestines. Our city deserved better.

It was my turn to come up with a suitable metaphor. Saying something original and creative had become more challenging at this point because we had gone through most of the body parts (the eyes, hands, at some point also the spleen). In the end, I settled for the feet because they symbolized movement, a going to and coming from somewhere. With more than 60 per cent of its residents having foreign roots, Brussels is the epitome of superdiversity. A polyglot place where everyone and no one feels at home. A dynamic city that welcomes a new influx of people every day, a place that is constantly being made and remade. My story had been one of movement as well: first from Ethiopia to Belgium when I emigrated to this country in 1995, then from Leuven to Brussels when I decided to move to the big city in my early twenties. The hegemony of white Flemish culture had started to suffocate me to the point that I had started curating myself as I tried to fit in with the dominant group. I was desperately craving for a new exciting, diverse environment that celebrated difference, where I could truly be myself and where there was no norm because everyone was the norm.

While describing Brussels it is challenging not to succumb to the clichés that inevitably float around every conversation about our country's capital. Perhaps it is impossible to find an adequate metaphor that truly captures the essence of this ephemeral city. Brussels is an amalgam of juxtapositions: a place that allows you to dream away on sultry summer nights, just to hit you with its rough reality the next day. I once read somewhere that Brussels is like the B side of a record page 179: not as glamorous as the catchy A side but the more you listened to it, the more you started to like its quirkiness, intimacy and originality. This couldn't be more true. When you live here you'll be amazed by its many gorgeous gardens and parks, art deco and art nouveau buildings in the most unexpected neighbourhoods, its raw authenticity and the way the scenery changes with every corner you turn. Brussels may not be as marketable as its neighbouring capital cities like Amsterdam and Paris, but it is a city that you slowly fall in love with until you can't imagine wanting to live anywhere else. However, it's a special kind of love, a kind of love that keeps you critical, a kind of love that keeps you questioning the space that you inhabit as you wonder how we as a community can do better. This atlas showcases the work of people who all share this kind of love for Brussels, depicting the diverging narratives and histories of different spaces, allowing us to dwell on the fascinating snapshots that make up this great city.

The challenge
Amina Saâdi

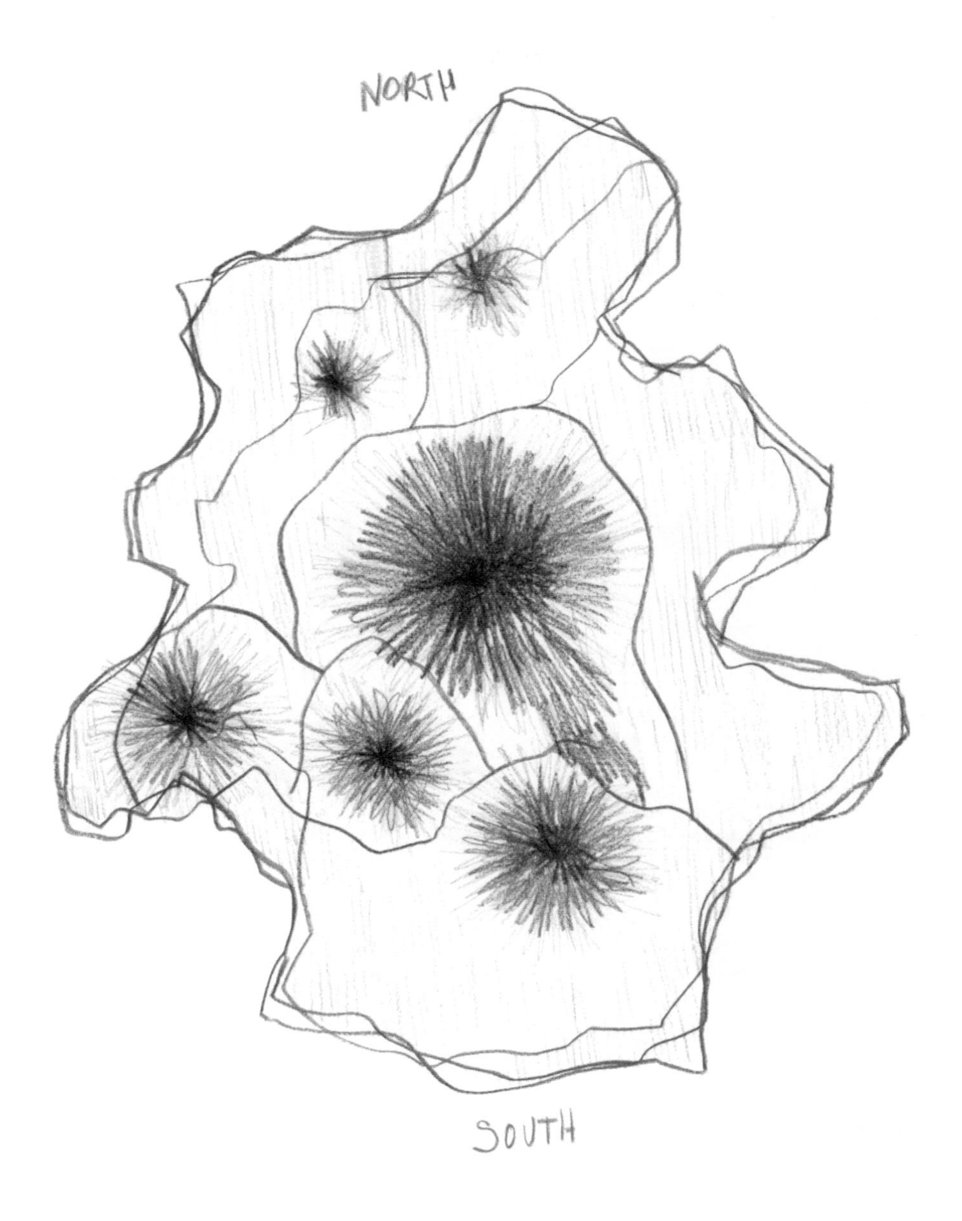

Cities in the city
Amina Saâdi

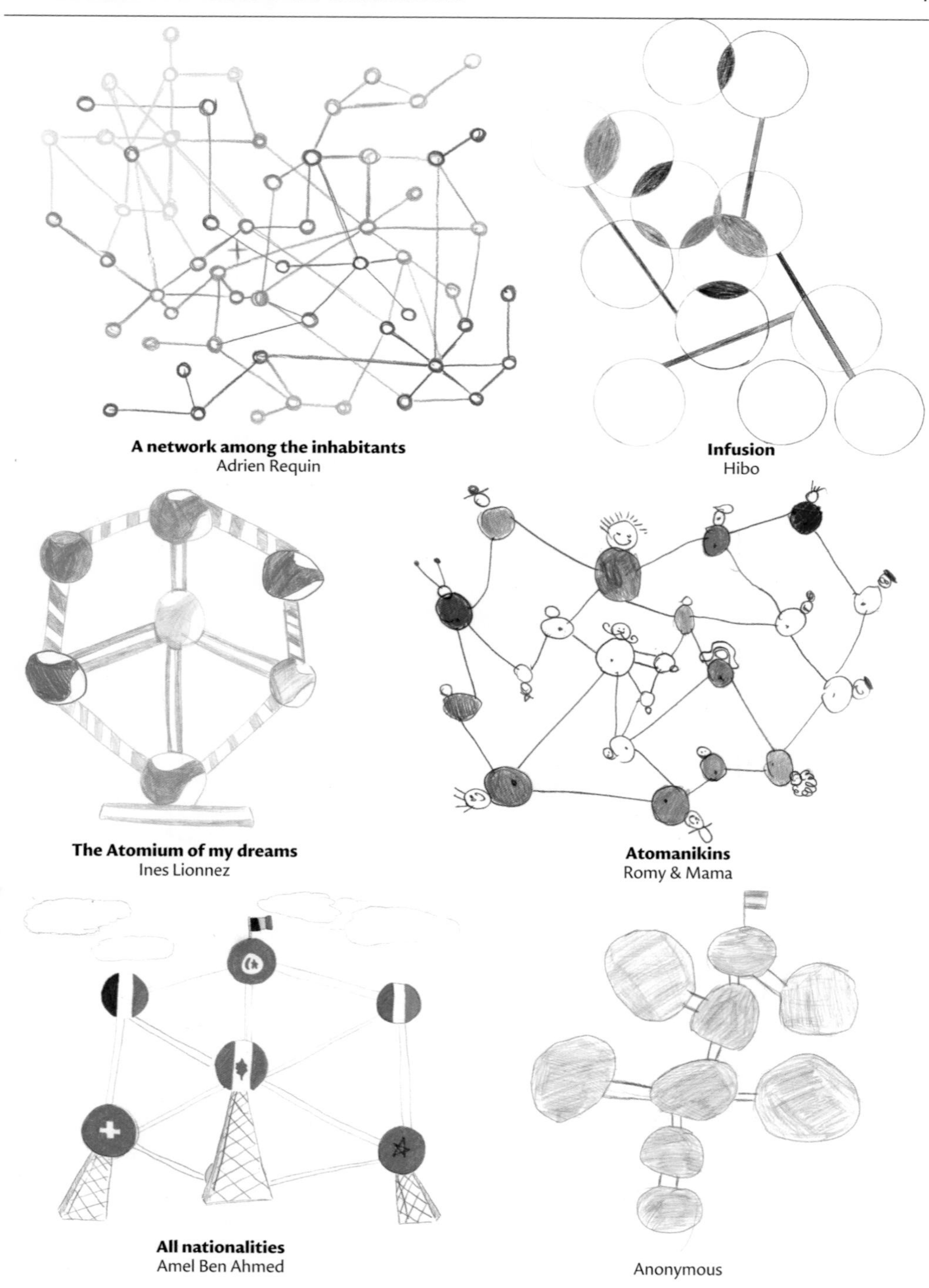

A network among the inhabitants
Adrien Requin

Infusion
Hibo

The Atomium of my dreams
Ines Lionnez

Atomanikins
Romy & Mama

All nationalities
Amel Ben Ahmed

Anonymous

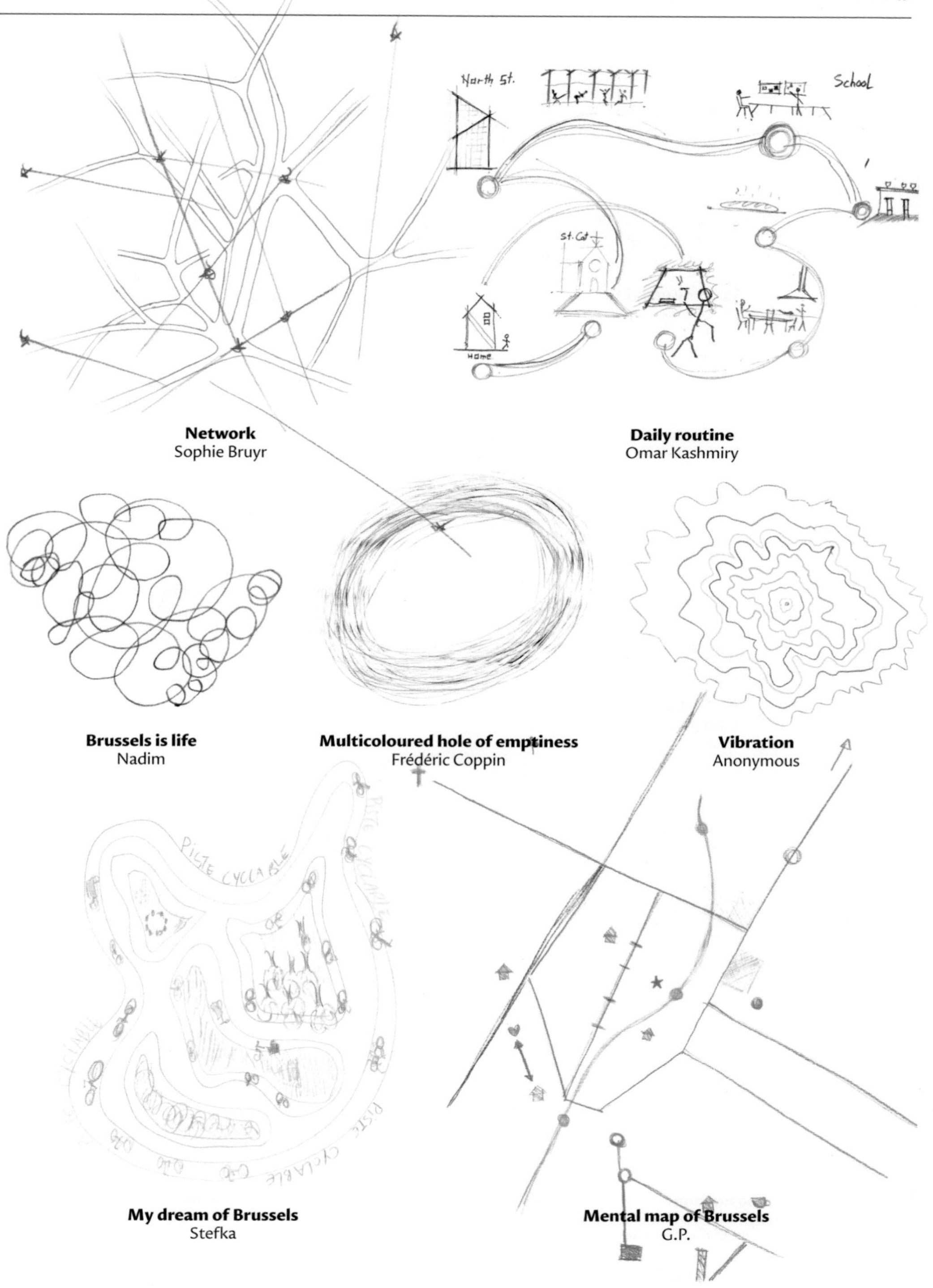

Network
Sophie Bruyr

Daily routine
Omar Kashmiry

Brussels is life
Nadim

Multicoloured hole of emptiness
Frédéric Coppin

Vibration
Anonymous

My dream of Brussels
Stefka

Mental map of Brussels
G.P.

So many people!
Bastien

Smoke
Silvy

Le Coq
Anonymous

There are those with umbrellas, and those without
Sandra

Where is the horizon?
Anonymous

Big tower & small house
Martha

After work in the park
Mathi Deveau

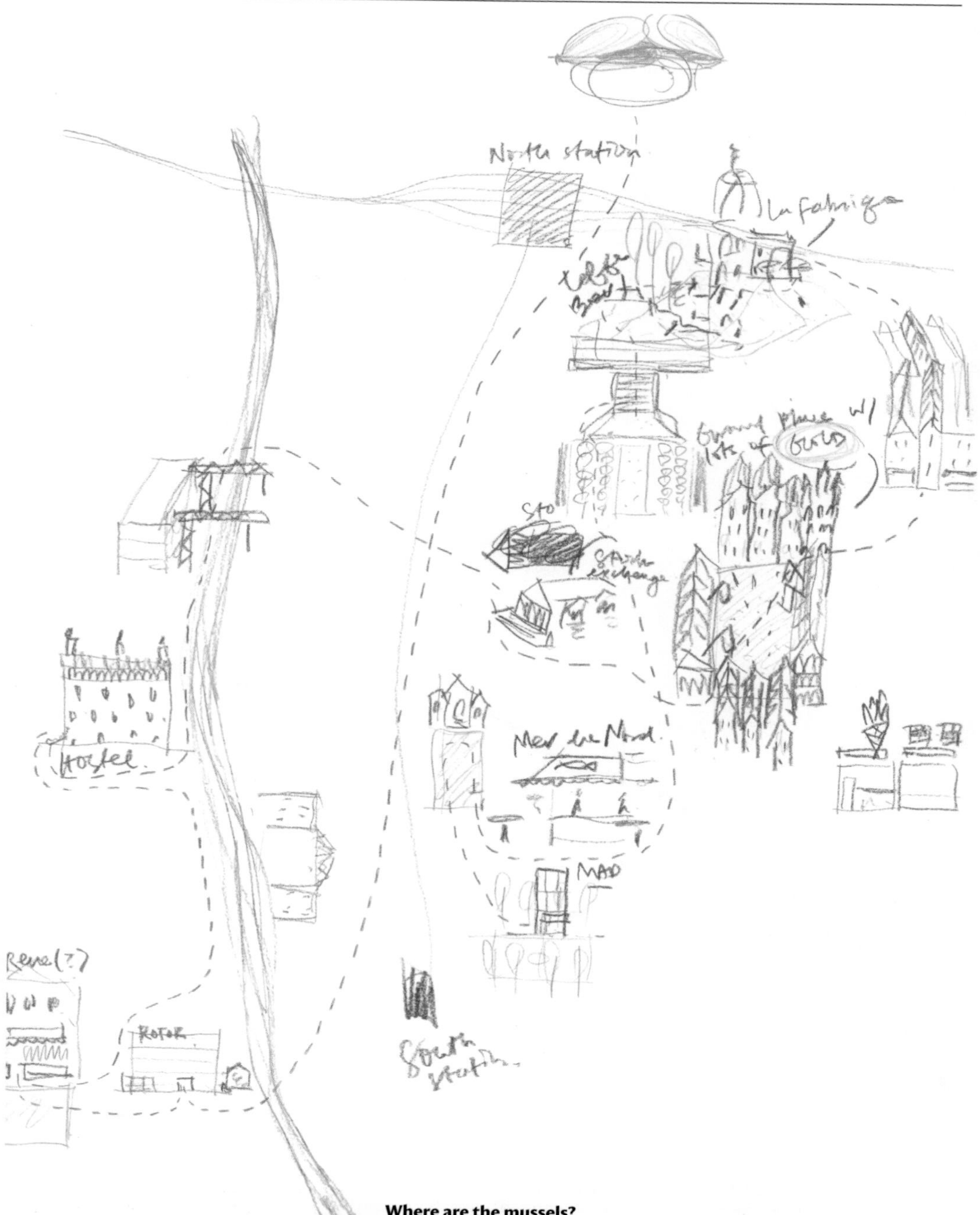

Where are the mussels?

The confusing but interesting journey of three tourists trying to find mussels in Brussels

Tanya

Omar Kashmiry

ME-TROPOLITAN

This map represents Brussels how – as an architecture student – I perceive it based on my daily routine and favourite spots. The dominant element is the railway that divides the city into two halves. The eastern half of the city is more elevated than the western part, which discourages me from going there by bike. The map focuses on the railway as the giant structure that cuts the city into two halves and questions its impact on the inhabitants.

Stijn Monsaert

VERSATILITY

Brussels stands out from other world capitals through its diverse international population and cultural plurality in a small but concentrated area. These infographics depict the demographic versatility between the different municipalities.

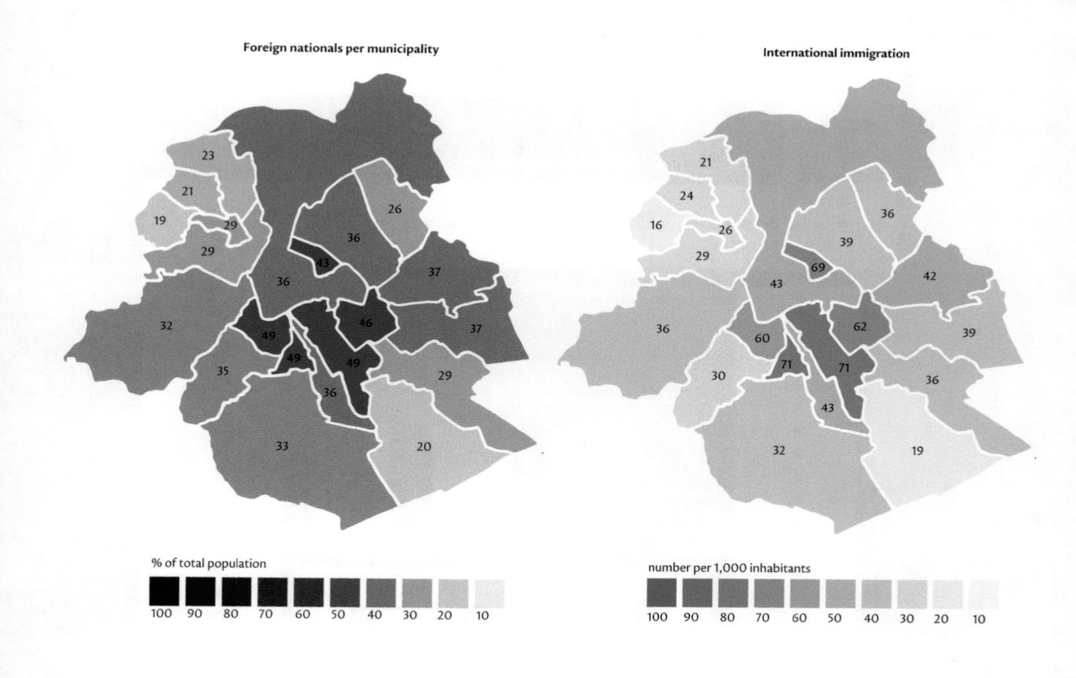

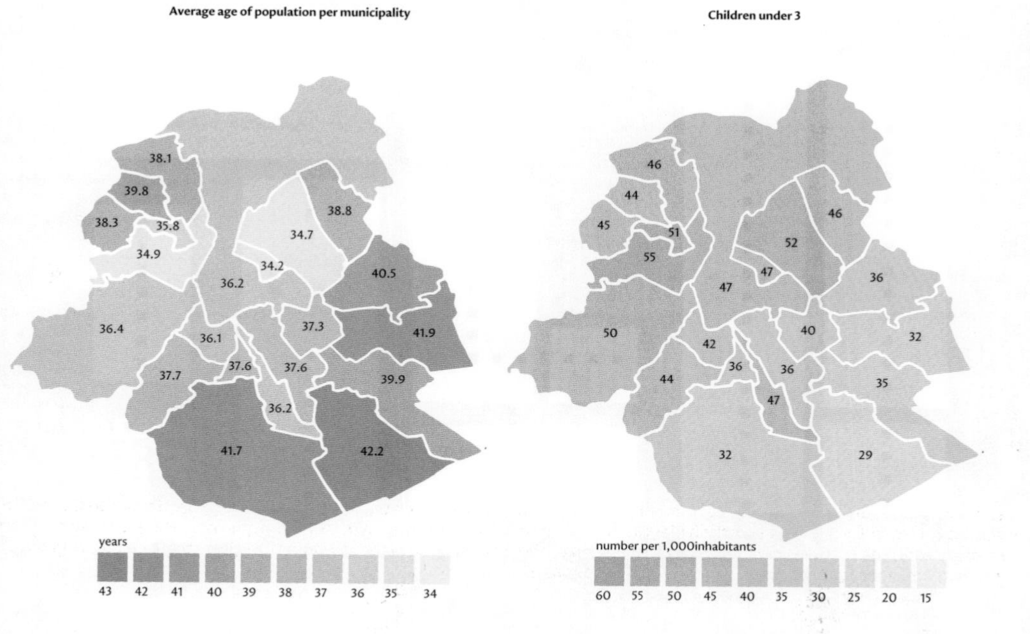

Source data: IBSA & SPF Economie - Statistics Belgium (RN)

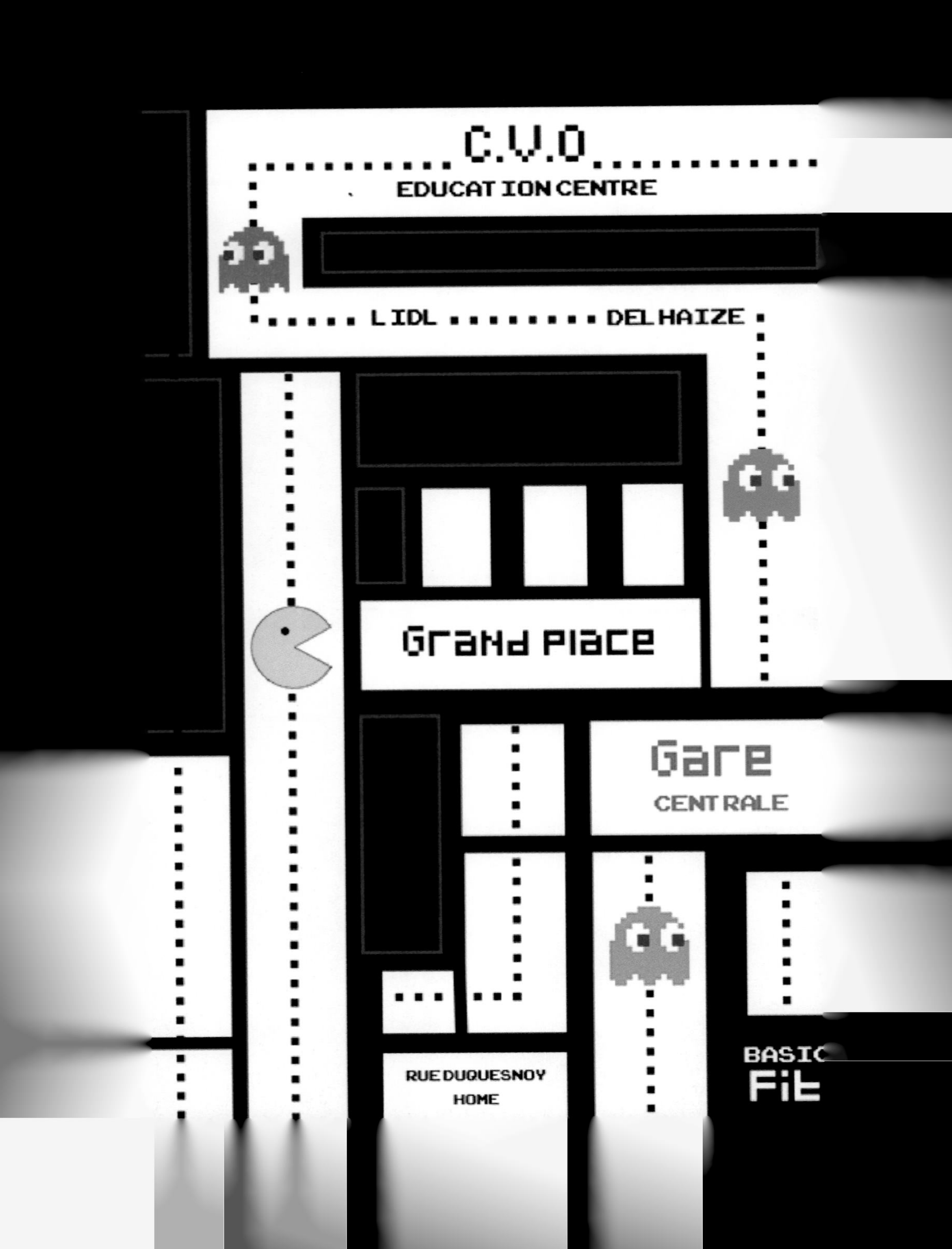
C.V.O
EDUCATION CENTRE
LIDL
DELHAIZE
Grand Place
Gare
CENTRALE
RUE DUQUESNOY
HOME
BASIC
Fit

Guido Bos

FAST LANE

BRUSSELS
BEEK
BY NIGHT
HOTEL
Hotel Deville
ZENIRUM
BEEK
TAXI
BXL
BOX
Parfait Palace Froidecoeur
Leugen PALEIS
if I had a ham
ICE BOX
BOITE de NUIT
ICE
Place Misère
fresh paint
modern museum
peinture fraîche
Cache Misère
LONDON
Send BOX
STU BRU
PARKING
Park King
HELSINKI
OFFICES 2 LET
CD
SHOP
IN Lobby OUT
OTTO CAR
TRIPLE TOUR BUS
Regers
Laat
I ♥ EU
Palace HOTEL
OUT of the box
thinking
Louiza
shoE shoP
Laan
Regers
bouchon
shoe man
square
ATHENA
TRIOMFB
MONTGOMERY
KLOK HUIS
Fado
Lord Monty
Juke
kick
Congo
square
triomphe
triumph
LISBOA
going
GO GO
MOUNT MERRY
GO
MOUNT MORRA
TUNNEL VISION
St Pieters
St Lambert
merry X-mas
happy
DOUBLE VISION
GOOGLE
BERG
BOX CAR
BOX OTTO
TAXI
ROBIN de ROBOT
STOCLET

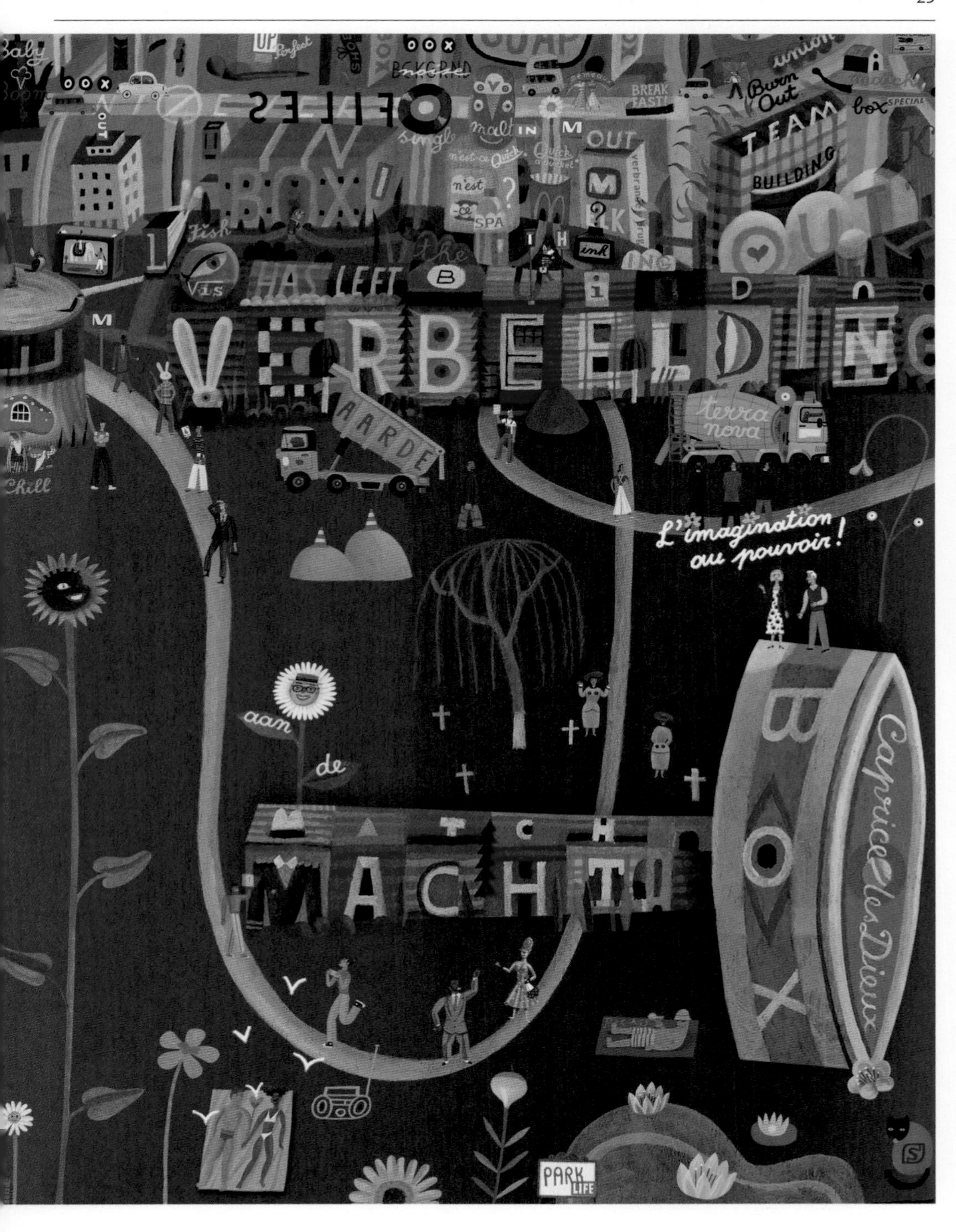
box
Burn Out
union
box
SPECIAL
BREAK FAST
TEAM
BUILDING
malt
IN
M
OUT
n'est-ce Quick
n'est -ce SPA
Fish
ink
Vis
HAS LEFT
B
AARDE
terra nova
Chill
L'imagination au pouvoir!
aan
de
Caprice des Dieux
BOX
MACHT
PARK LIFE

Lente 2016
De dag dat het ZONLICHT niet meer scheen
BRAIN Storm Weather
MIND MAP
MIND THE GAP!
ne faisons pas d'AMALGAME
2 MUCH? INFORMATION
the Ensor, my friend, is blowin' in the wind.
BELGICA
avec la mer du nord
comme dernier terrain vague
ATLANTIKWALL
le plat pays qui est le mien
nouvelle vague
OVER STROMING
1000 BOMMEN & GRANATEN
in Flanders Fields
ochtend humor
BEEK
cité modèle
molenbeek
NOT IN MY NAME
NOT IN MY BACKYARD
CANAL
SPIEGEL PALEIS
PALEIS SPIEGEL
GARE du NORD
à la gare comme à la gare
Laken
FAILED STATE
GOOGLE BERG
Via duc
TUNNEL VISION
DOUBLE VISION
COMP(L)OT theorieën
CANAL+
KARL MARX
NIET VERDWALEN!
BORDER colleague
onder BUIK
BEEK
It takes 2 2 tango!
ASBAK
NIGHT SHIFT
NACHT PLOEG
NIGHT
AIR
HELMET St.
hond
SHOCKED
KRUIT FABRIEK
hond met hoed
Juke box
EU
Alle Menschen werden Brüder
NEON Judgement
MINI EUROPE
parlementair onderzoek
le massacre du printemps
BRUSSELSE STEINWAY
Kan Kunst de Wereld redden?
COMPLEX CITY!
you are here
Warande
Daar bij die molen...
KUNST
ARTS
SPA
Reine
Elisabeth
Concours
Liber
l'égalité
Fraternité
Eternité
Froidecœur
BELLE VUE
Slow Cooking
vismet
mitraillette
COUSCOUS KRETEN
porte de Ninove
ALLAHOE SNACKBAR
Zwarte vijver

avec un ciel si gris qu'il faut lui pardonner
Here comes the Sun
SocAir
Imagine
imaginair
& NOreligion 2
ACHT MUSIK
NIGHT
VISION AIR
à COLORIER!
Somewhat over the top
Virgin suicide bomber
Solidair
Salut, maman.
Somewhere over the rainbow...
Don't
OVER DRIVE
humidité
avec un ciel si bas qu'il fait l'humanité
BRUSSEL
TAX Free
Brussels
BYNIGHT
allemaal lichtjes
man met hoedje
ochtendtumor
LUCHT HAVEN TEM
HEBBEN EM
SABYNA
Airport
GLOBAL
WARNING
LEGO LAND
NATO
OTAN
E19
BANANA REPUBLICA
J'AI VU
HELSINKI
OVER DREVEN
MEDIA
TELE VISIE
TELE VISION
STOP STAR WARS
Stockholm Syndrome
VERBEELDING MACHT
MOUNT GO MARRY
Global
B
BB
the final COUNT DOWN
Place Misère
HOTEL
momo
NOITE
BCKGRND
FACTO
SHOCKED
Lobby
CLEAN TEAM
etter BEEK
WAKE UP
MAKE UP
going going to a to a GO GO GO GO
TOP DOWN
SARDINE ASPIRINE
INTER ROGER
Brussels
SPIEGEL PALEIS
PALEIS SPIEGEL
LOCK DOWN
à quoi culture
à quoi bon?
Juste ici? PALEIS
RADIO ACTIV
SPOOK STAD
I'm here
ceci n'est pas l'empire de la lumière
THE HATER OF HATE
Vive me liberté
Bruxelles ma belle?
het rijk der verlichting
no irony
BELLE VUE
moder museum
CHOCOLALALA
Deze stad wil men helpen, maar dan is 't om zeep liefst
je suis Charlie
Who's CHARLIE
KUNST BERG
Bozar
XXL
BOITE NUIT
Napo Leon
WATER L'EAU
BRUSSEL CENTRAL
La fille en rose
La vie en rose(s)
POPUP
Chill
Ball of confusion
Bal van de Burgemeester
Ho Lee
30°
WHAT?
HAPPENING
INSIDE
BEURS
SHARIA
SYRIË
M

What is my vision of the City of Brussels? For answering this question we were invited to realize an artistic and geographical project: to accompany the inhabitants of several neighbourhoods in the realization of their own map of the City of Brussels. During several creative residencies at various locations we created a series of subjective maps together with the local residents.

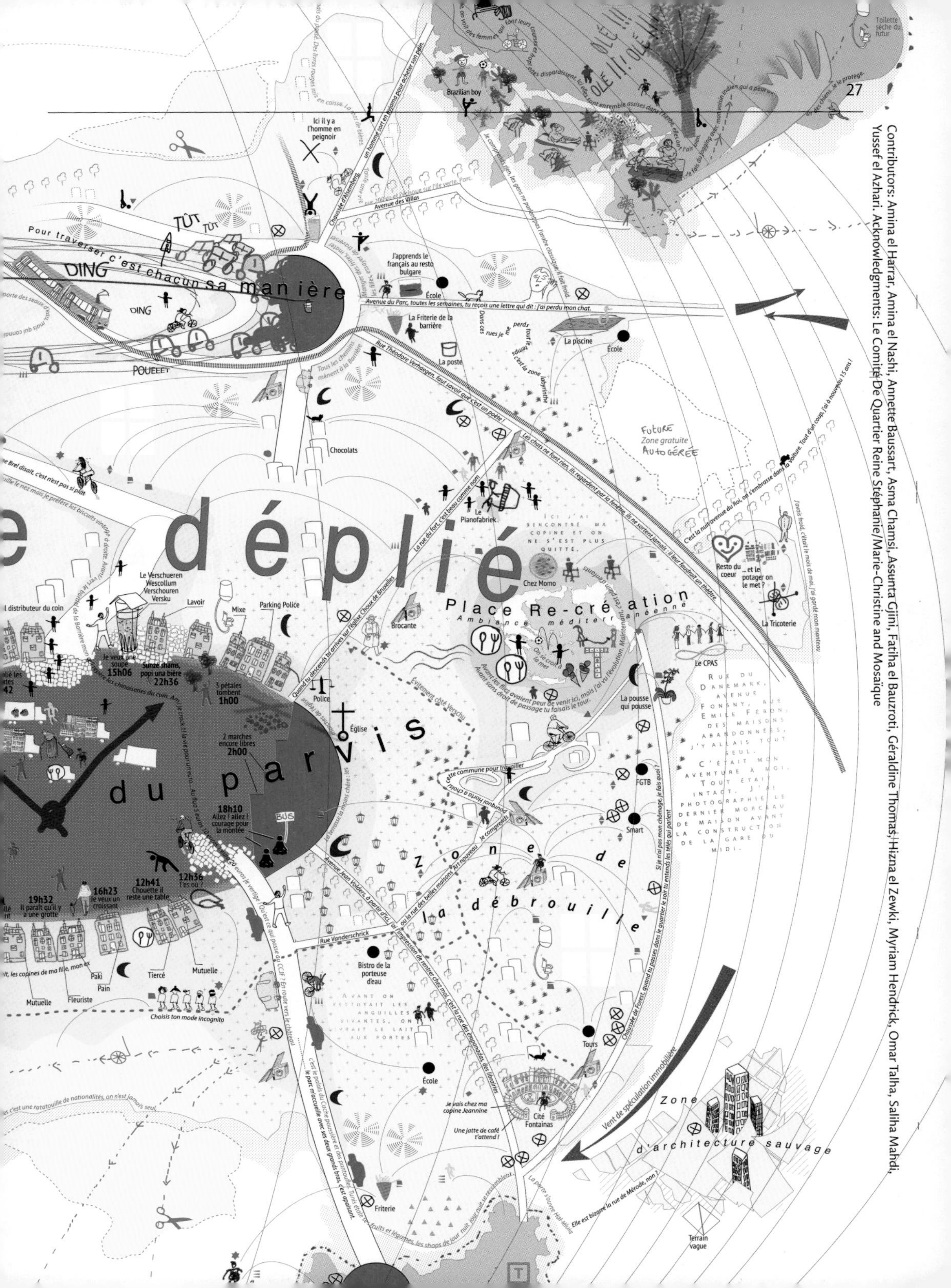

Contributors: Amina el Harrar, Amina el Nashi, Annette Baussart, Asma Chamsi, Assunta Gjini, Fatiha el Bauzroti, Géraldine Thomas, Hizna el Zewki, Myriam Hendrick, Omar Talha, Saliha Mahdi, Yussef el Azhari. Acknowledgments: Le Comité De Quartier Reine Stéphanie/Marie-Christine and Mosaïque

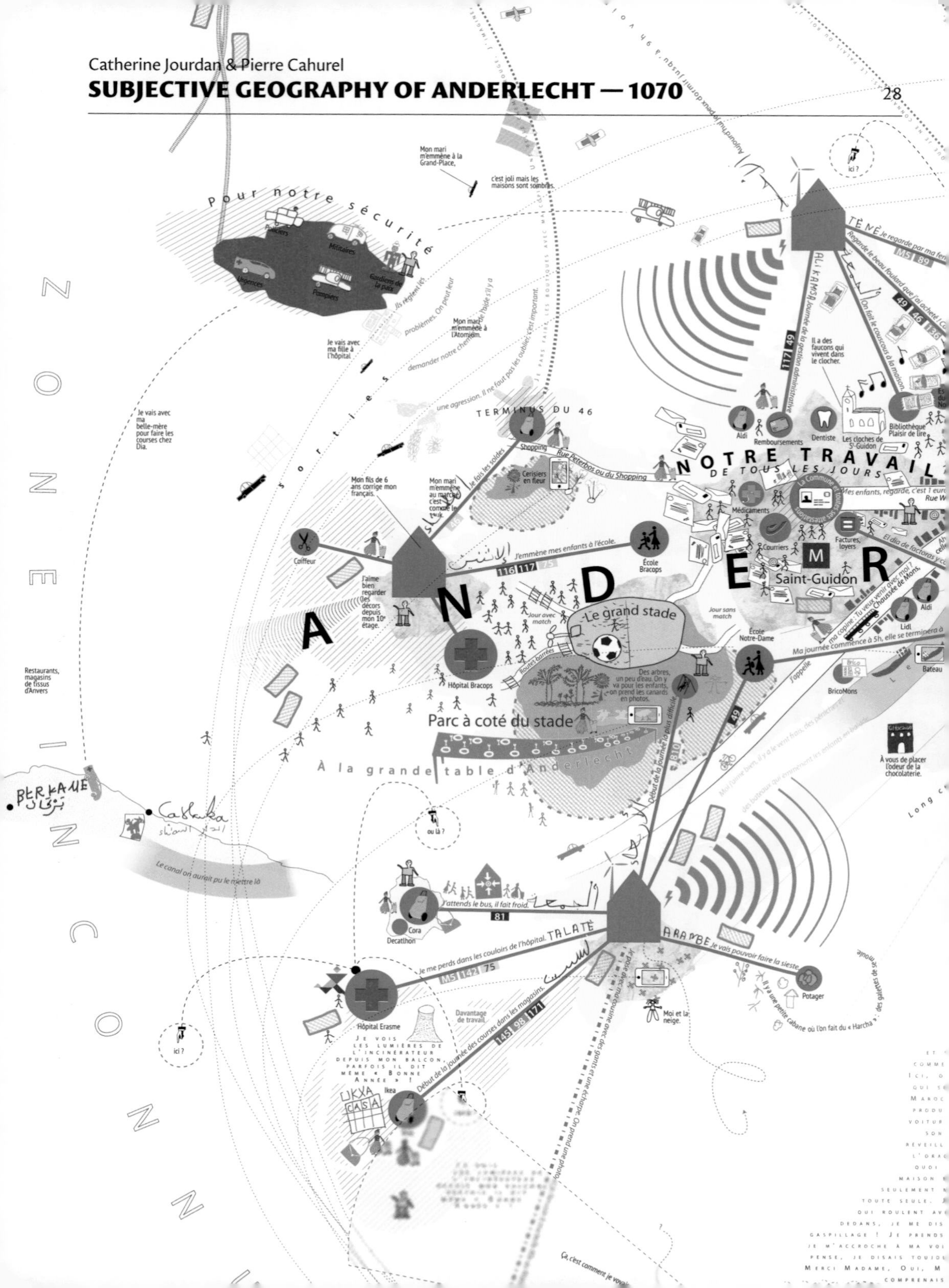
Mon mari m'emmène à la Grand-Place,
c'est joli mais les maisons sont sombres.
Pour notre sécurité
Policiers
Militaires
Urgences
Pompiers
Gardiens de la paix
Ils règlent les problèmes. On peut leur demander notre chemin, de l'aide s'il y a une agression. Il ne faut pas les oublier, c'est important.
Mon mari m'emmène à l'Atomium.
Je vais avec ma fille à l'hôpital
sorties
Je vais avec ma belle-mère pour faire les courses chez Dia.
TERMINUS DU 46
Shopping
Rue Peterbos ou du Shopping
Cerisiers en fleur
Je fais les soldes
Mon fils de 6 ans corrige mon français.
Mon mari m'emmène au marché, c'est comme le ...
Coiffeur
J'emmène mes enfants à l'école.
École Bracops
116 117 75
J'aime bien regarder les décors depuis mon 10e étage.
A N D E R
Jour avec match
Le grand stade
Jour sans match
Hôpital Bracops
Routes barrées
Des arbres, un peu d'eau. On y va pour les enfants, on prend les canards en photos.
Parc à coté du stade
À la grande table d'Anderlecht
Début de la journée la plus difficile
École Notre-Dame
Ma journée commence à 5h, elle se terminera à ...
Restaurants, magasins de tissus d'Anvers
ZONE INCONNUE
ou là ?
ici ?
Le canal on aurait pu le mettre là
J'attends le bus, il fait froid.
81
Cora
Decathlon
TALATÉ
ARAYBE
Je vais pouvoir faire la sieste.
Potager
Il y a une petite cabane où l'on fait du « Harcha », des galettes de semoule
Je me perds dans les couloirs de l'hôpital.
MS 142 75
Hôpital Erasme
Davantage de travail.
Début de la journée des courses dans les magasins.
145 98 171
JE VOIS LES LUMIÈRES DE L'INCINÉRATEUR DEPUIS MON BALCON, PARFOIS IL DIT MÊME « BONNE ANNÉE » !
Ikea
Moi et la neige.
Je joue avec ma cousine avec des gants et une écharpe. On prend une photo.
Ça, c'est comment je voyais...
NOTRE TRAVAIL DE TOUS LES JOURS
Aldi
Remboursements
Dentiste
Les cloches de St-Guidon
Bibliothèque Plaisir de lire
Il a des faucons qui vivent dans le clocher.
Médicaments
Courriers
Factures, loyers
La Commune et toutes ses attestations
M
Saint-Guidon
Mes enfants, regarde, c'est 1 euro
Ma copine : Tu veux venir avec moi ?
Chaussée de Mons,
Aldi
Lidl
BricoMons
Bateau
J'appelle
À vous de placer l'odeur de la chocolaterie.
TÈNÈ Je regarde par ma fenêtre
Regarde le beau foulard que j'ai acheté !
On fait le couscous à la maison.
ALI KAMS Journée de la gestion administrative
117 49
MS 89
49 46 136
Aujourd'hui je peux dormir jusqu'à 9h voir...
BERKANE
Casablanca

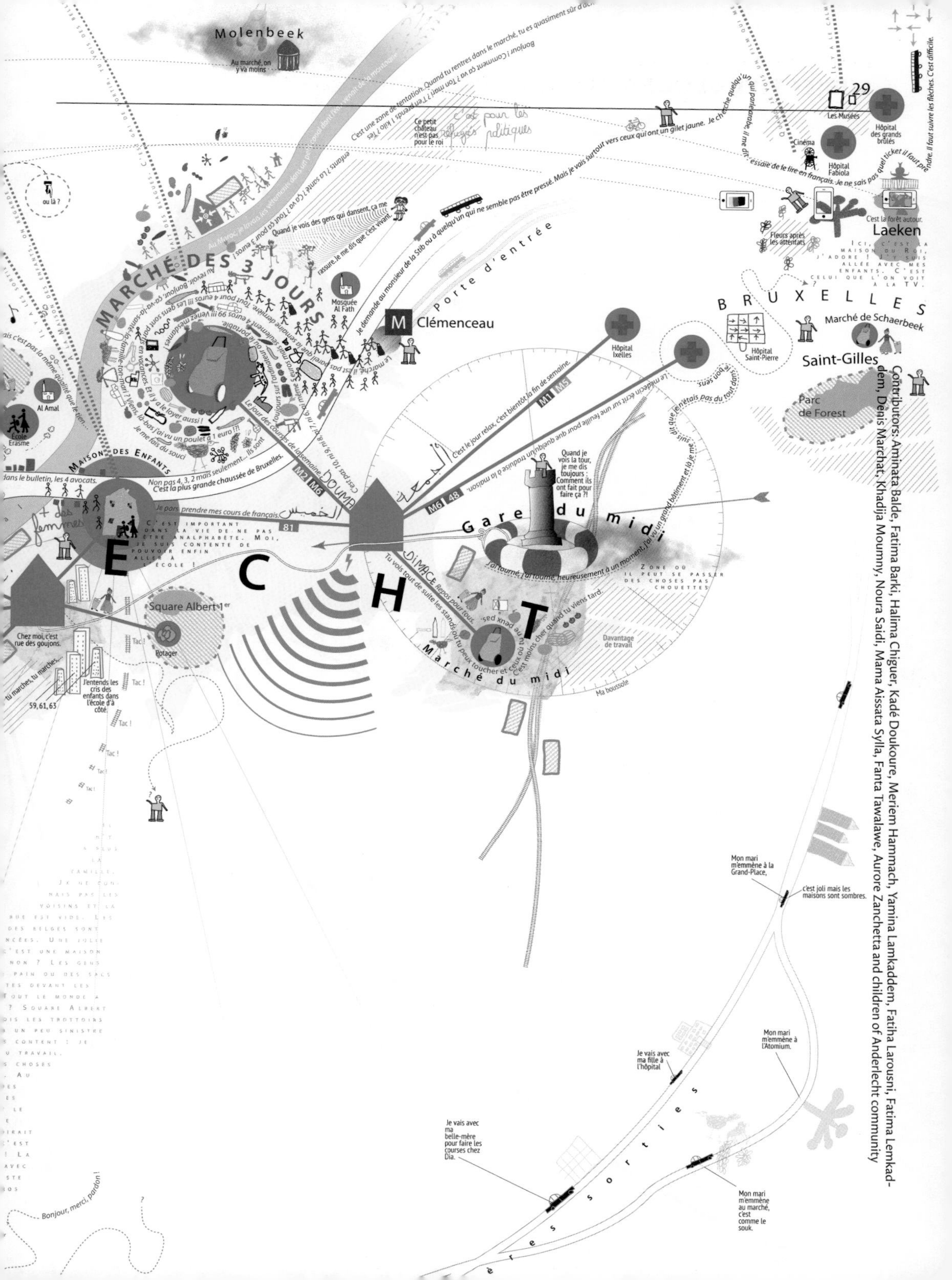

Molenbeek
Au marché, on y va moins
Ce petit château n'est pas pour le roi
C'est pour les réfugiés politiques
Les Musées
Hôpital des grands brûlés
Cinéma
Hôpital Fabiola
C'est la forêt autour.
Laeken
Ici, c'est la maison du Roi, j'adore ! J'y suis allée avec mes enfants. C'est celui que l'on voit à la TV.
Fleurs après les attentats
BRUXELLES
Marché de Schaerbeek
Saint-Gilles
Parc de Forest
Hôpital Saint-Pierre
Hôpital Ixelles
Mosquée Al Fath
Clémenceau
porte d'entrée
MARCHÉ DES 3 JOURS
Quand je vois des gens qui dansent, ça me rassure. Je me dis que c'est vivant.
Al Amal
École Erasme
Maison des Enfants
C'est la plus grande chaussée de Bruxelles.
Non pas 4, 3, 2 mais seulement... Ils sont
Je pars prendre mes cours de français.
C'est important dans la vie de ne pas être analphabète. Moi, je suis contente de pouvoir enfin aller à l'école !
ECHT
Square Albert 1er
Chez moi, c'est rue des goujons.
Potager
J'entends les cris des enfants dans l'école d'à côté.
Tac !
59, 61, 63
Quand je vois la tour, je me dis toujours : Comment ils ont fait pour faire ça ?!
Gare du midi
J'ai tourné, j'ai tourné, heureusement à un moment, j'ai vu un grand bâtiment et là je me suis dit que je n'étais pas du tout perdue.
Zone où il peut se passer des choses pas chouettes
C'est le jour relax, c'est bientôt la fin de semaine.
Davantage de travail
Marché du midi
Ma boussole
M1 M5
M2 M6
M6 48
81
Mon mari m'emmène à la Grand-Place,
c'est joli mais les maisons sont sombres.
Mon mari m'emmène à l'Atomium.
Je vais avec ma fille à l'hôpital
Je vais avec ma belle-mère pour faire les courses chez Dia.
Mon mari m'emmène au marché, c'est comme le souk.
ères sorties
Bonjour, merci, pardon !
Contributors: Aminata Balde, Fatima Barki, Halima Chiguer, Kadé Doukoure, Meriem Hammach, Yamina Lamkaddem, Fatiha Larousni, Fatima Lemkaddem, Denis Marchat, Khadija Moumny, Noura Saidi, Mama Aissata Sylla, Fanta Tawalawe, Aurore Zanchetta and children of Anderlecht community

Catherine Jourdan & Pierre Cahurel

SUBJECTIVE GEOGRAPHY OF LAEKEN — 1020

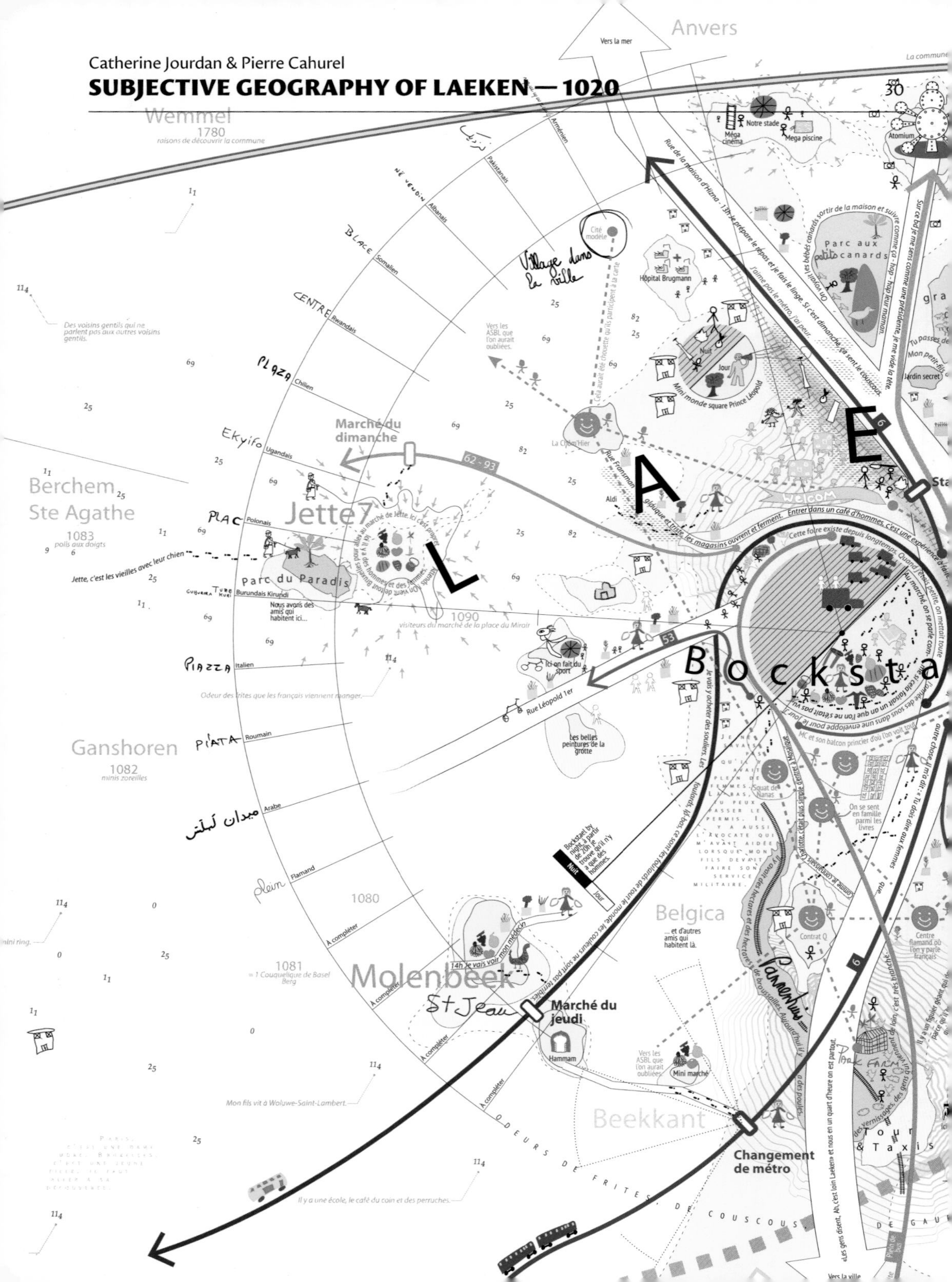

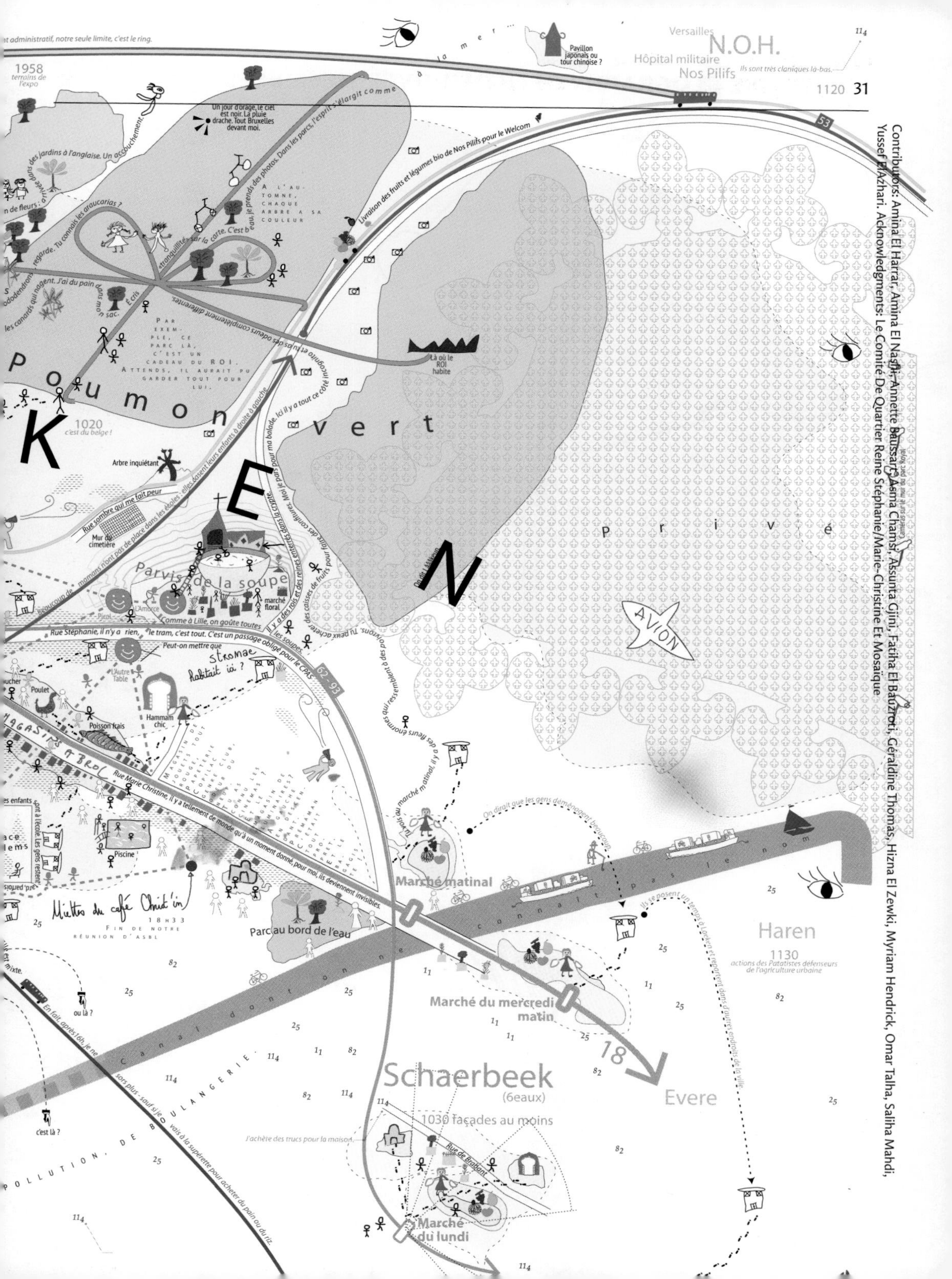

Contributors: Amina El Harrar, Amina El Nasiri, Annette Buissart, Asma Chamsi, Assunta Gjini, Fatiha El Bauzroti, Geraldine Thomas, Hizna El Zewki, Myriam Hendrick, Omar Talha, Saliha Mahdi, Yussef El Azhari. Acknowledgments: Le Comité De Quartier Reine Stéphanie/Marie-Christine Et Mosaïque

Le roi est là
Il est pas là
Ligne de bus fantôme
En fait ici c'est Laeken
Joseph y est allé 7 fois : 1 fois pour la médaille, 6 fois pour réparer le lave-linge.<<
Passage clandestin
casse-vitesse... ralentisse
Ring scolaire
Chemin des moutons romains. Mini via ovis romàne.
Et si on en faisait un palais ?
Écoles
Boerderij
Je suis un vieux de 1922
Forê
Versailles
Blokkendozen
rue de la villa au toit de paille
Rue du serpent de jonquilles
Rue de la victoire de Brabant
Avenue des « mal-traités de Versailles »
Plus à gauche, non plus à droite
Zone à faire revivre / Nieuw leven inblazen
EN 14/18, LE PROPRIÉTAIRE GARDAIT DES PORCS. L'UN D'ENTRE EUX ÉTAIT ENGRAISSÉ « AU NOIR » POUR SA PROPRE FAMILLE. ET QUAND LES VOISINS DEMANDAIENT S'IL AVAIT BIEN DÉCLARÉ TOUS LES PORCELETS, SA RÉPONSE ÉTAIT TOUJOURS : JE SUIS UN BON BELGE. LES HABITANTS L'ONT APPELÉ « DE BELCH ».
C'ÉTAIT NÉGLISE DE LA RÉUNIFICATION ? JA, DAS WAAR ALORS ILS AURAIENT PU FAIRE UN EFFORT
Des lecteurs entrent et sortent
Bibliothèque
Les gens discutent à travers leurs chiens « et toi ton chien comment il va ? »
Ben Hur «Sauveur de la poste»
MQ Rossignol à faire vivre
Patate Straat - La Grand Rue et notre unique place
Familia Gemeenschapscentrum
Grand bain
Utopia
ZAVELPUT
Rue des écoles
Ongevallenlaan
Grande rue des accidents
Rue des batailles avec des Louis
Parc dis
Le cresson sur rail
La rampe de lancement des navetteurs
Rue de la montée des bus
Si on met les églises on met aussi la mosquée et les Black Star
Marais
Ici y a rien pour l'instant
L'enfer des autos
AL'AMOUR
en als we eens gewoon aarde maken in plaats van ons groen afval te verbranden in de verbrandingsoven ?
Port de plaisance
Niveau de la mer

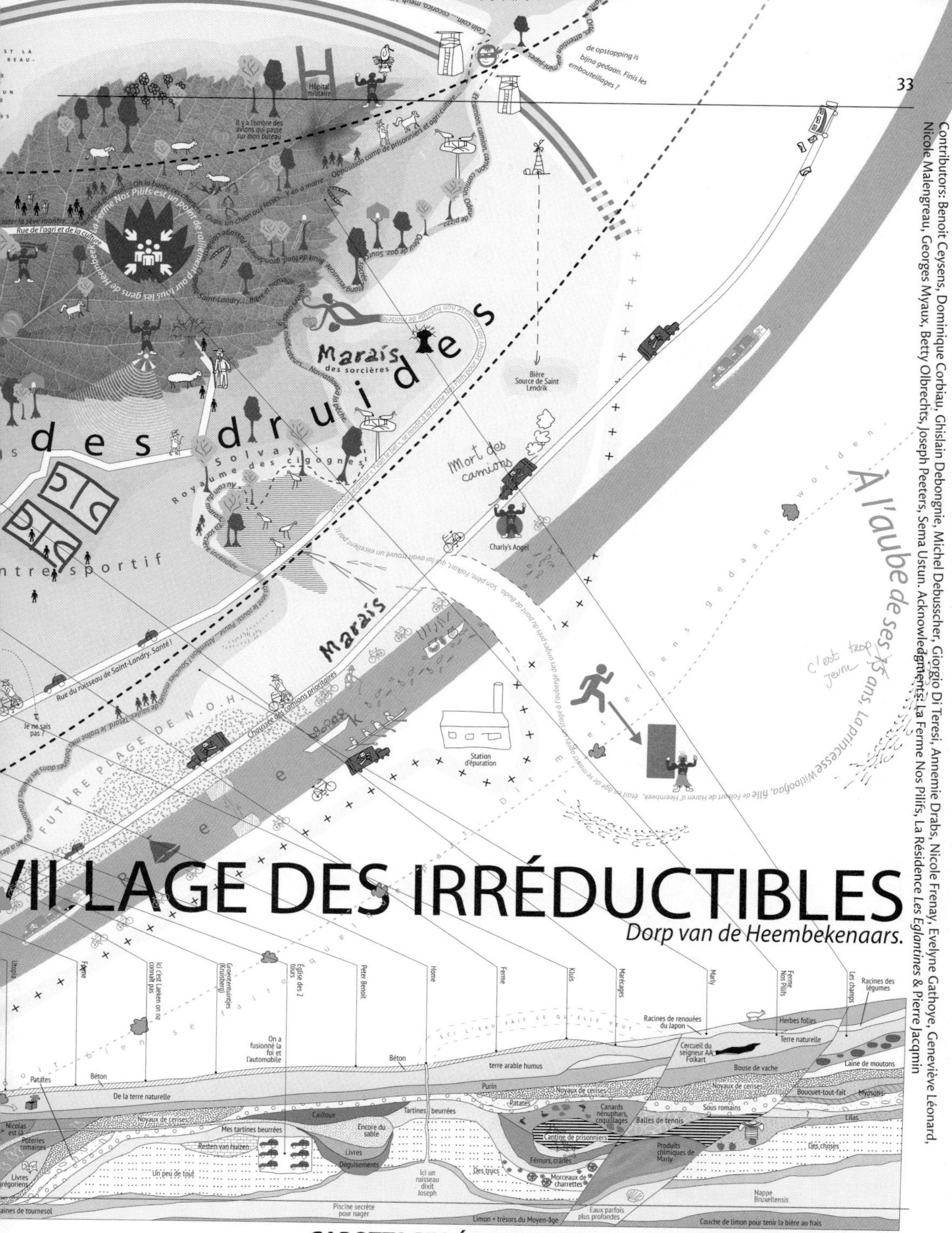

CAROTTAGES ÉQUIVOQUES DE NEDER-OVER-HEEMBEEK

Contributors: Benoit Ceysens, Dominique Corbiau, Ghislain Debongnie, Michel Debusscher, Giorgio Di Teresi, Annemie Drabs, Nicole Frenay, Evelyne Gathoye, Geneviève Léonard, Nicole Malengreau, Georges Myaux, Betty Olbrechts, Joseph Peeters, Sema Ustun. Acknowledgments: La Ferme Nos Pilifs, La Résidence *Les Eglantines* & Pierre Jacqmin

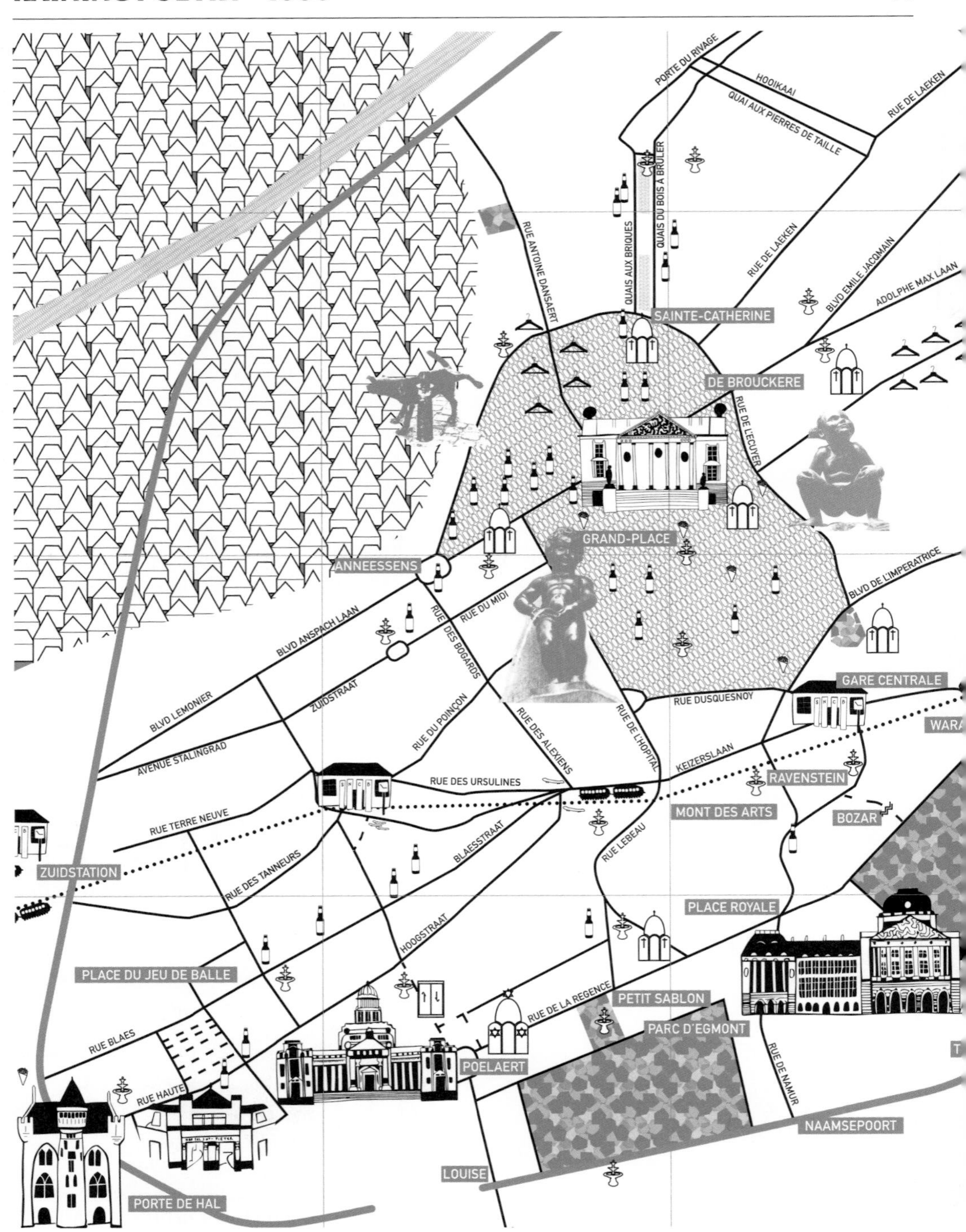
PORTE DU RIVAGE
HOOIKAAI
QUAI AUX PIERRES DE TAILLE
RUE DE LAEKEN
QUAIS DU BOIS A BRULER
QUAIS AUX BRIQUES
RUE ANTOINE DANSAERT
RUE DE LAEKEN
BLVD EMILE JACQMAIN
ADOLPHE MAX LAAN
SAINTE-CATHERINE
DE BROUCKERE
RUE DE L'ECUYER
GRAND-PLACE
ANNEESSENS
BLVD DE L'IMPERATRICE
RUE DU MIDI
RUE DES BOGARDS
BLVD ANSPACH LAAN
ZUIDSTRAAT
BLVD LEMONIER
RUE DU POINÇON
RUE DES ALEXIENS
RUE DE L'HOPITAL
RUE DUSQUESNOY
GARE CENTRALE
AVENUE STALINGRAD
RUE DES URSULINES
KEIZERSLAAN
RAVENSTEIN
MONT DES ARTS
BOZAR
RUE TERRE NEUVE
ZUIDSTATION
RUE DES TANNEURS
BLAESSTRAAT
RUE LEBEAU
PLACE ROYALE
HOOGSTRAAT
PLACE DU JEU DE BALLE
RUE DE LA REGENCE
PETIT SABLON
PARC D'EGMONT
RUE BLAES
POELAERT
RUE DE NAMUR
RUE HAUTE
NAAMSEPOORT
LOUISE
PORTE DE HAL

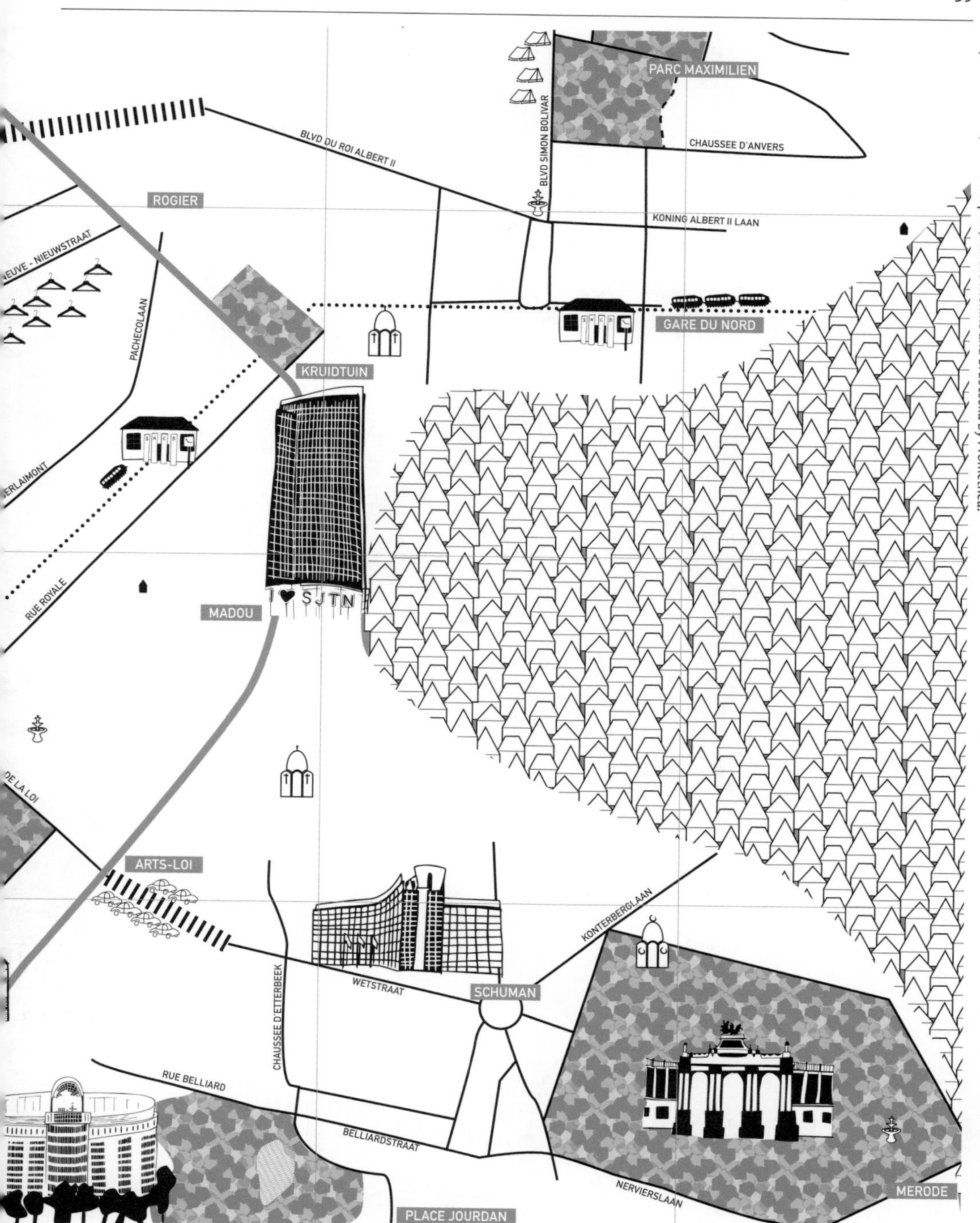

For Peauésie, aka Raining Poetry, poems are placed in the streets of Brussels. Poems are invisible when the ground is dry and are revealed by water. This project is a collaboration with ERG, Sophie Daxhelet, Piknik Graphic, Karelle Menine and Bruocsella by Promethea.

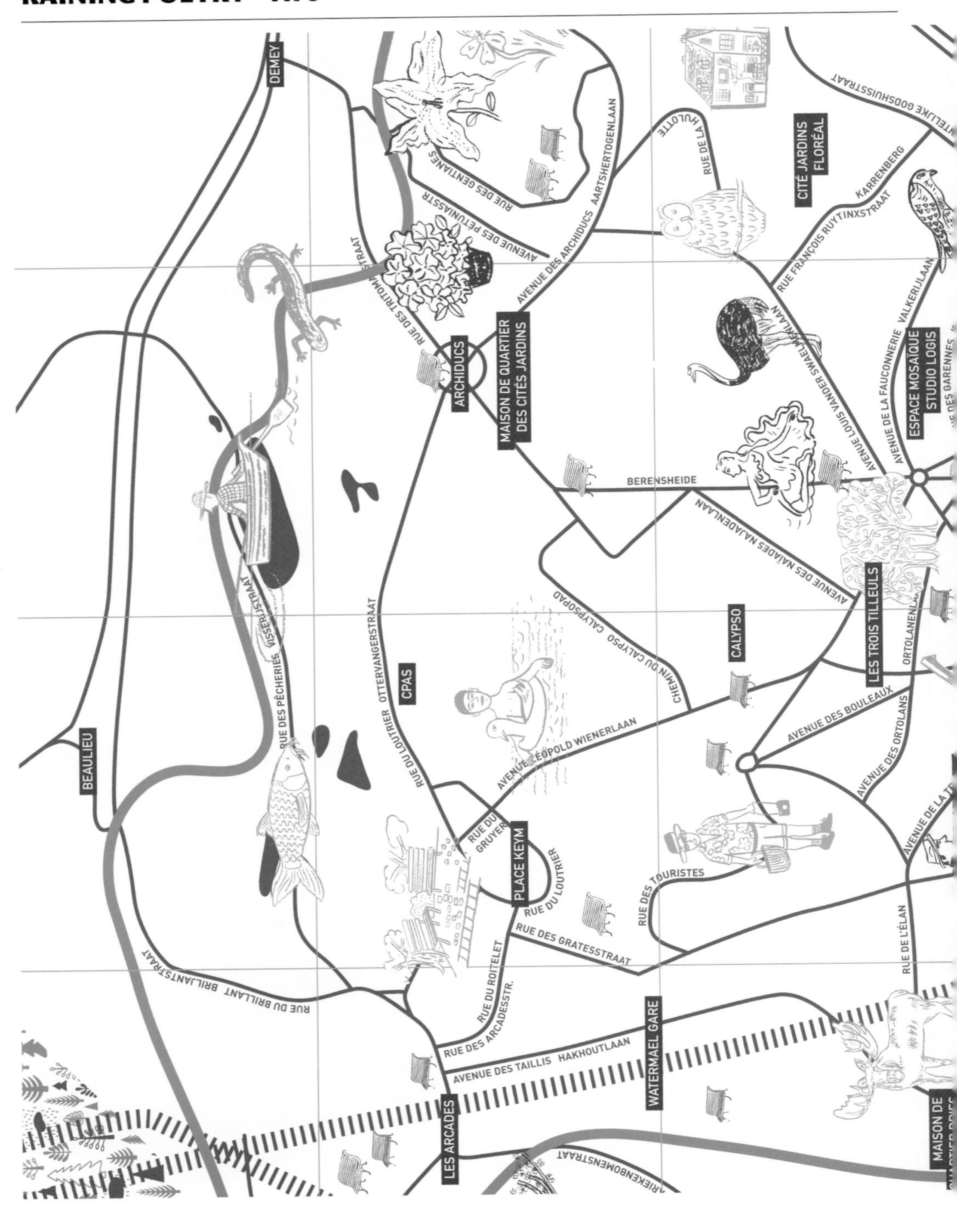
DEMEY
BEAULIEU
LES ARCADES
WATERMAEL GARE
PLACE KEYM
CPAS
ARCHIDUCS
MAISON DE QUARTIER DES CITÉS JARDINS
CALYPSO
LES TROIS TILLEULS
CITÉ JARDINS FLORÉAL
ESPACE MOSAÏQUE STUDIO LOGIS
RUE DES GENTIANES
AVENUE DES PÉTUNIAS
AVENUE DES ARCHIDUCS AARTSHERTOGENLAAN
RUE DE LA HULOTTE
KARRENBERG
RUE FRANÇOIS RUYTINXSTRAAT
AVENUE LOUIS VANDER SWAELMENLAAN
AVENUE DE LA FAUCONNERIE VALKERIJLAAN
BERENSHEIDE
AVENUE DES NAÏADES NAJADENLAAN
CHEMIN DU CALYPSO CALYPSOPAD
AVENUE LÉOPOLD WIENERLAAN
RUE DU LOUTRIER OTTERVANGERSTRAAT
RUE DES PÊCHERIES VISSERIJSTRAAT
RUE DU GRUYER
RUE DU LOUTRIER
RUE DES TOURISTES
RUE DES GRATESSTRAAT
AVENUE DES BOULEAUX
AVENUE DES ORTOLANS
ORTOLANENLAAN
RUE DE L'ÉLAN
RUE DU BRILLANT BRILJANTSTRAAT
RUE DU ROITELET
RUE DES ARCADESSTR.
AVENUE DES TAILLIS HAKHOUTLAAN

For Peauésie, aka Raining Poetry, poems are placed in the streets of Brussels. Poems are invisible when the ground is dry and are revealed by water. This project is a collaboration with ERG, Sophie Daxhelet, Piknik Graphic, Karelle Menine, Anne Versailles and Bruocsella by Promethea.

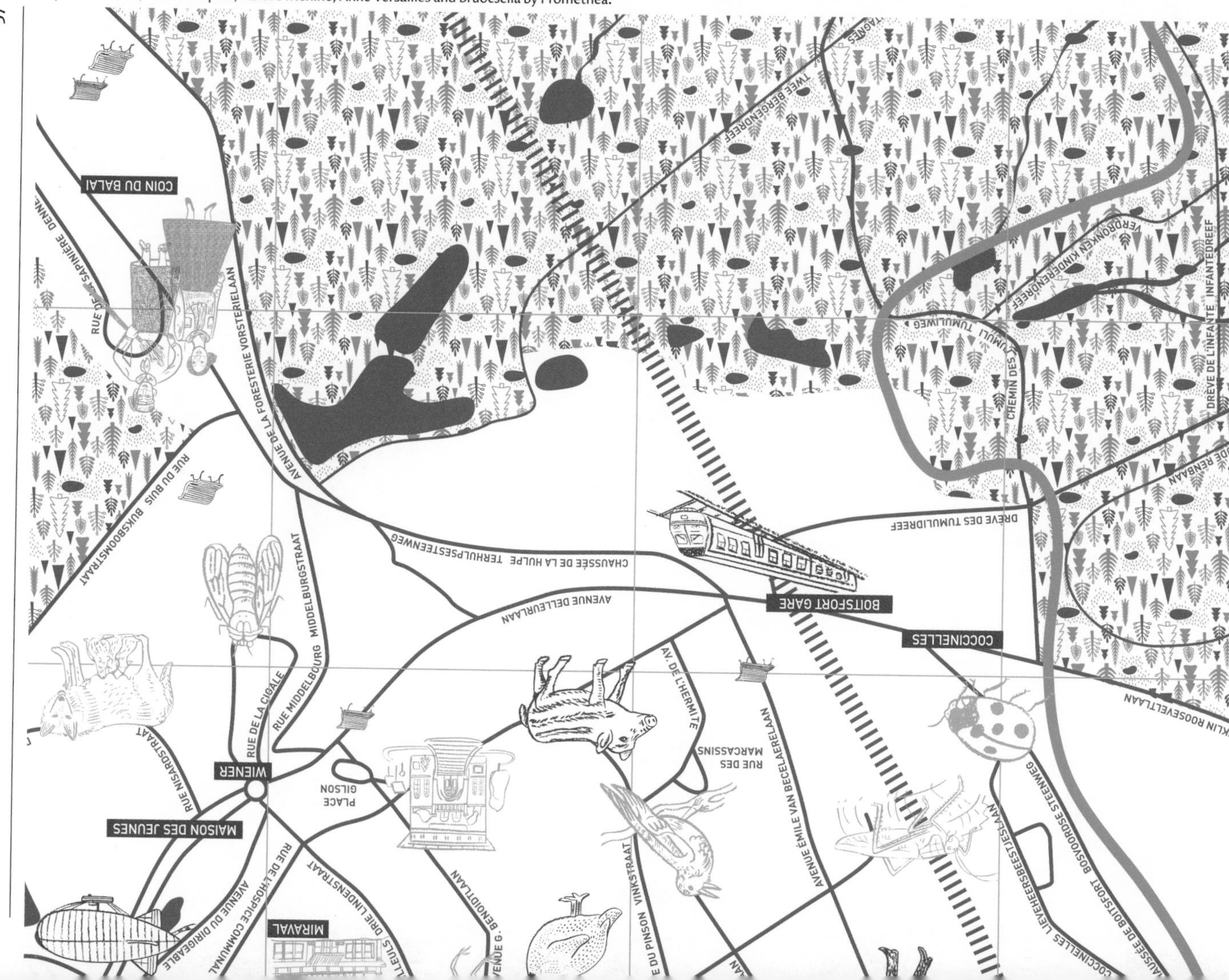

Liselore Lisemarie Margrit

Margaux Simouna Dena

Anonymous B. Noppe Pierre

Pieterjan
Lewis
Laetitia
Caillaud
Bastien
Lotte
Arnaux
Margrit
Lisemarie

The secondary river valleys of Brussels have given the city its characteristic traits.
Ecole Mondiale's ambition is to transform its nineteenth-century shape into
a twenty-first-century version that is based on its particular hydrographical structure.
Ecole Mondiale is working around the transition from the old nineteenth-century political model
towards an alternative vision for a metropolitan landscape by giving more power to the secondary river valleys.

Map 1837

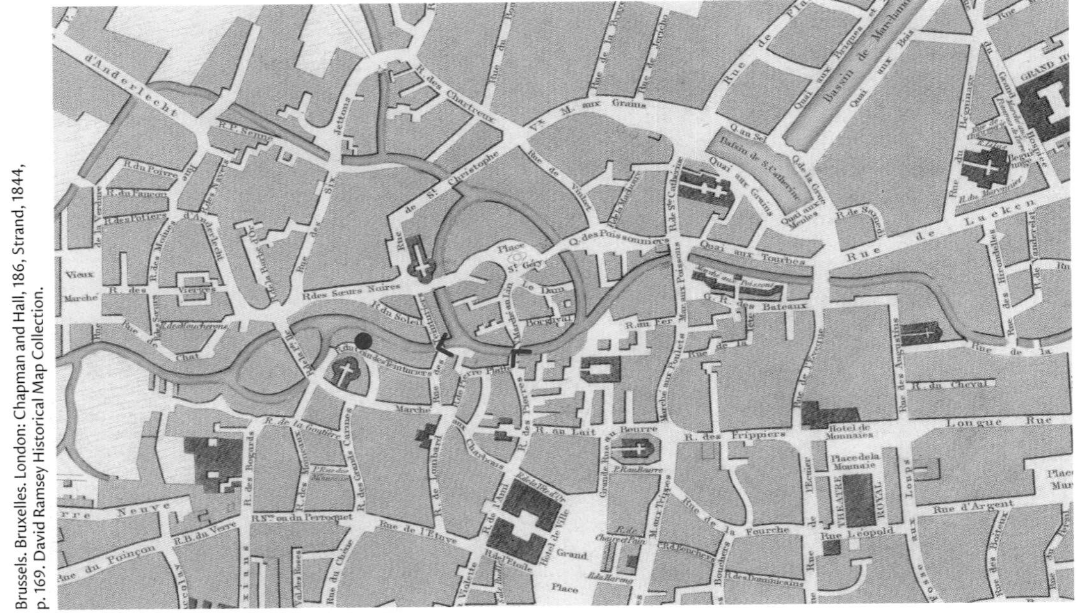

Map before the covering of the Senne, 1837

Brussels. Bruxelles. London: Chapman and Hall, 186, Strand, 1844, p. 169. David Ramsey Historical Map Collection.

Map 2018

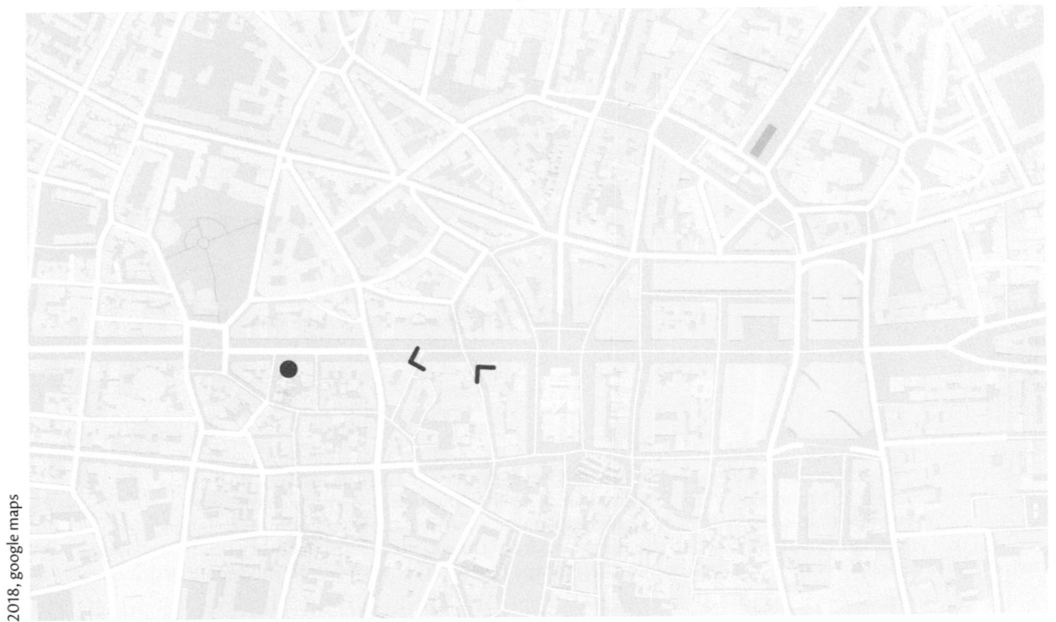

Current map of Boulevard Anspach and its surroundings

● Where I live, longing for the Senne...

2018, google maps

Senne view 1837

View from the bridge at Rue des Teinturiers, upstream

View from the bridge at Rue des Pierres, upstream

Street view 2018

View in the same direction as the above picture, 2018

View in the same direction as the above picture, 2018

KANAALTOCHTEN
BRABANT
JENITA

SITA
SITA
Jost Group
HAVILAND

DOCKS BRUXSEL
Anixton

R S.N.B.
1874
U N.B.

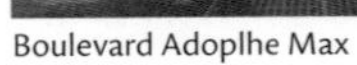

Boulevard Adoplhe Max

Rue de la Sablonnière

Place de la Liberté

Rue de Bériot

Rue de Namur

Rue Haute

Rue Limnander

Rue Saint Alphonse

Rue Teniers

Rue des Drapiers

Avenue des Azaleas

Chaussée d'Etterbeek

Chaussée de Louvain

Rue Neuve

Rue Saint-Quentin

Rue du Saint-Esprit

Rue des Poissonniers

Botanique

In this graphic you can see the level of satisfaction that I experience every day while biking to work. The measurements were made on a random sunny day in spring.

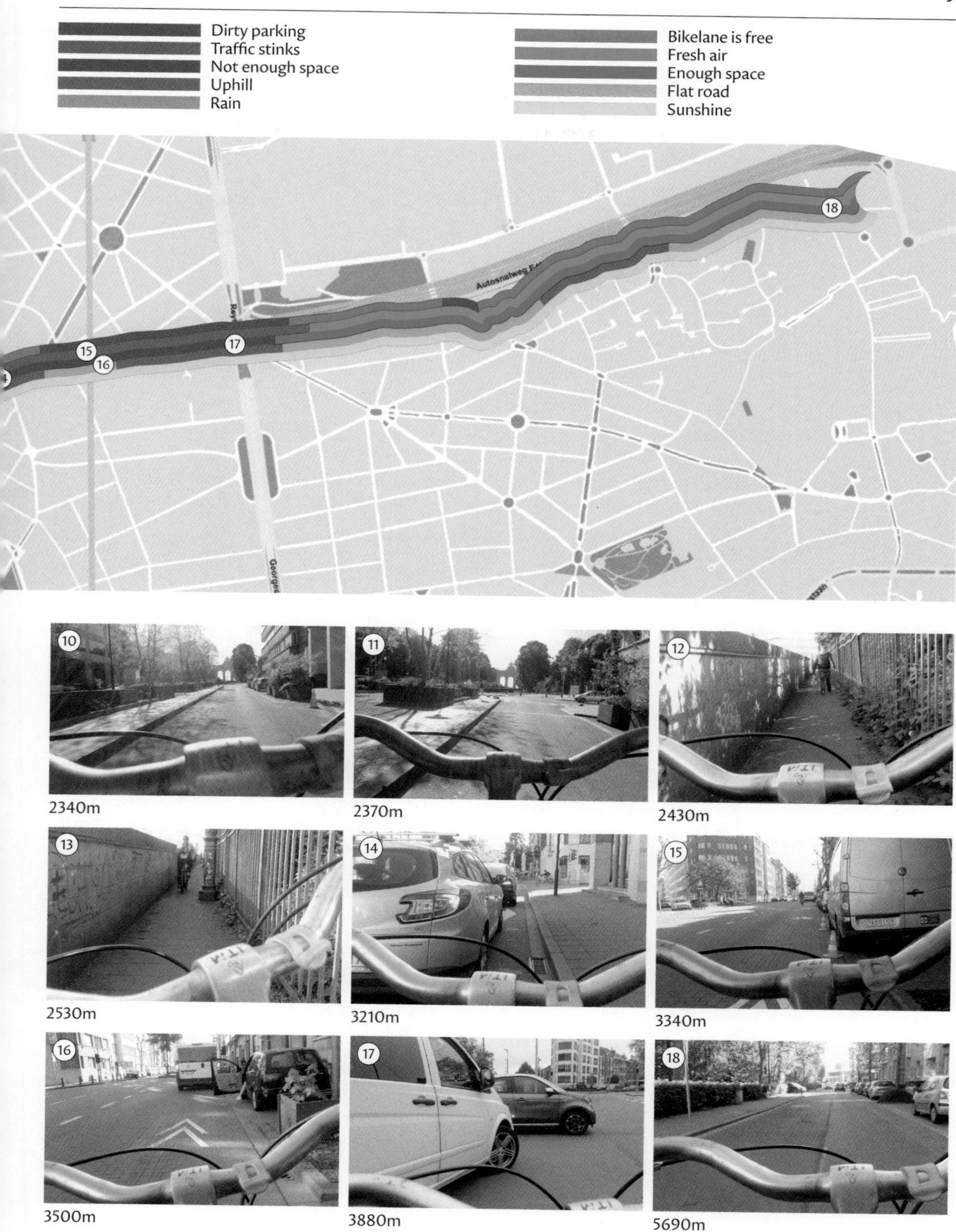

Map: www.mybrugis.irisnet.be. Service Name: Brugis WMS. EPSG:31370. Belgian Lambert 72

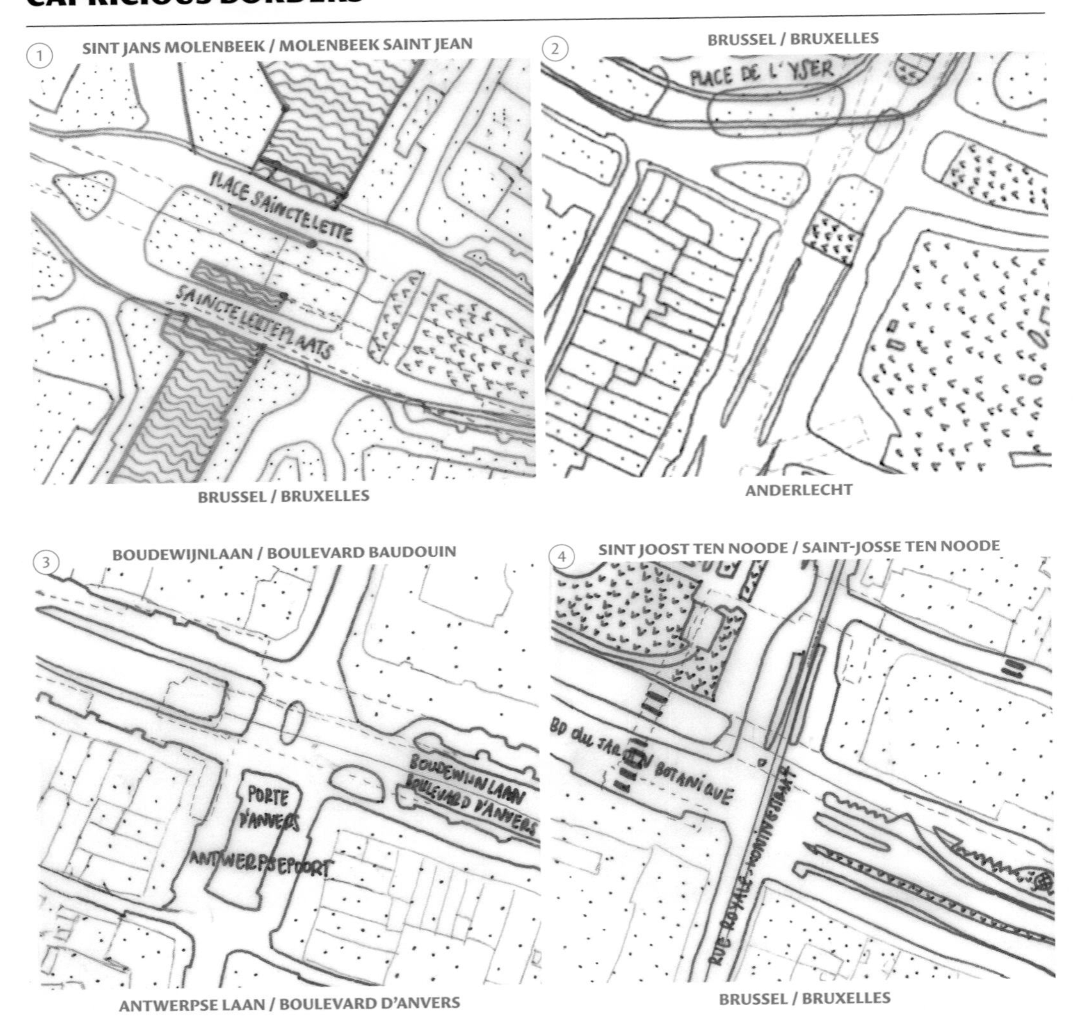

Every big city is a complex puzzle of private and public territories. More than anywhere else, Brussels seems endlessly divided, fractured between communal, regional, federal and private territories. Every day and completely without our knowledge, we cross these invisible borders.

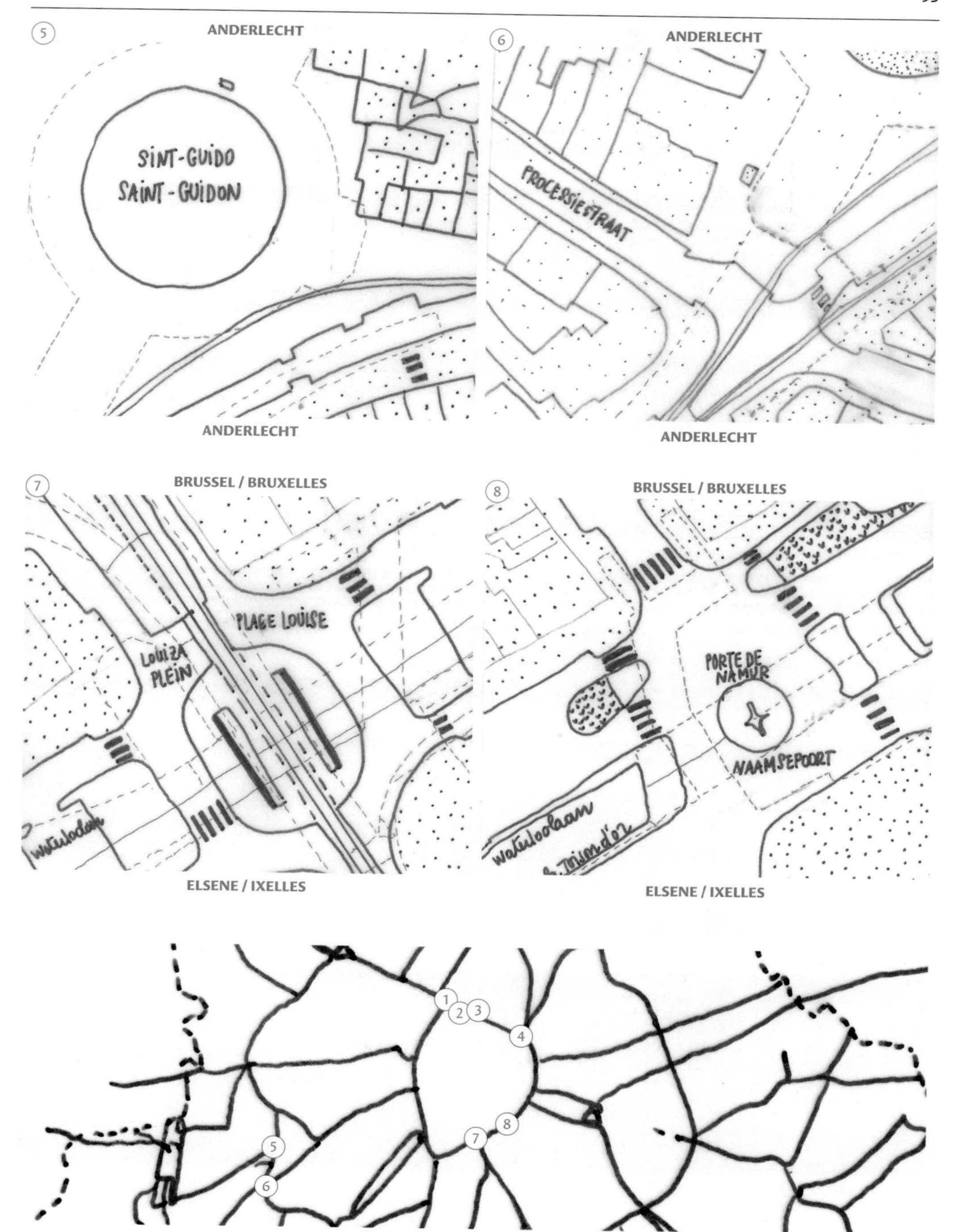
5
ANDERLECHT
SINT-GUIDO
SAINT-GUIDON
ANDERLECHT
6
ANDERLECHT
PROCESSIESTRAAT
ANDERLECHT
7
BRUSSEL / BRUXELLES
PLACE LOUISE
LOUIZA PLEIN
ELSENE / IXELLES
8
BRUSSEL / BRUXELLES
PORTE DE NAMUR
NAAMSEPOORT
waterloolaan
ELSENE / IXELLES
1
2
3
4
5
6
7
8

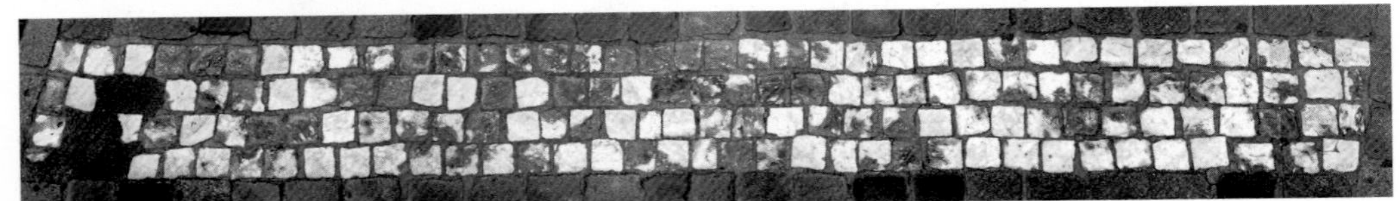

Forest, Rue du Curé * Chaussée de Bruxelles

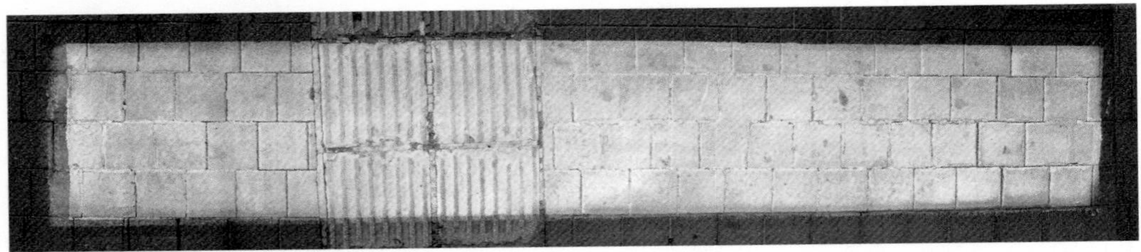

Brussels, Rue du vieux marché aux Grains

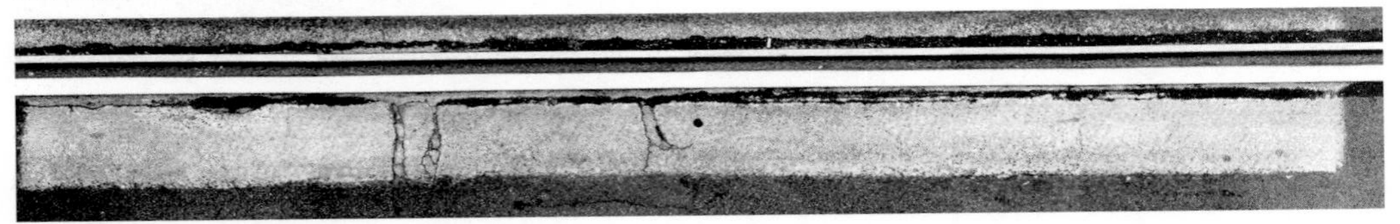

Schaerbeek, Rue des Palais * Rue de la Marne

Saint-Gilles, Gare Midi

Saint-Josse, Rue du Progrès

Uccle, Rue Victor Allard

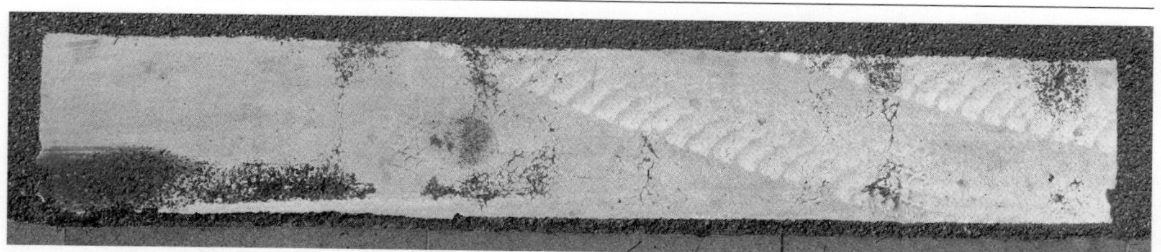

Watermael, Avenue du Dirigeable

Ixelles, Avenue de la Couronne

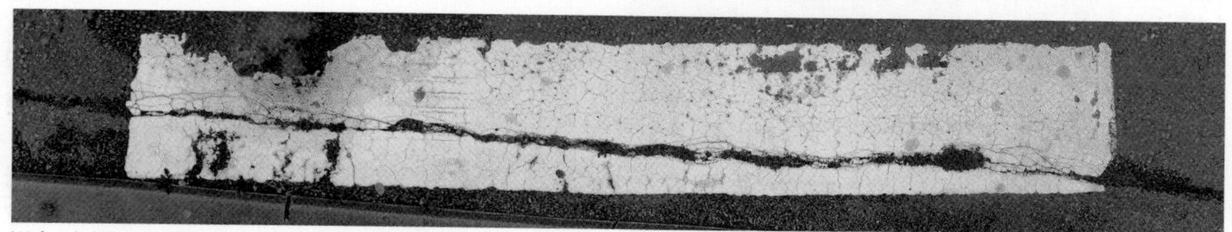

Woluwé-Saint-Lambert, Rue Dries * Rue du Carrefour

Auderghem, Rue Valduc

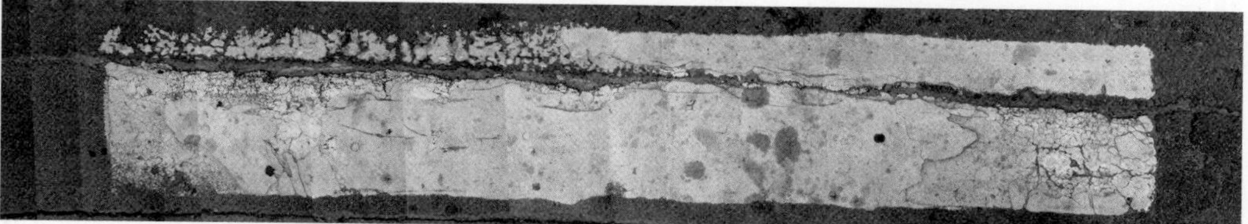

Etterbeek, Place Jourdan

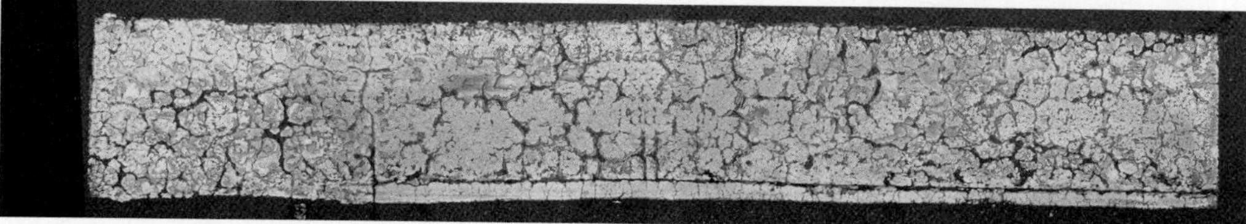

Auderghem, avenue Henri de Brouckère

DOORGANG
VOETGANGERS
ONDERBROKEN
HANDELAARS
BEREIKBAAR
PASSAGE PIETONS
INTERROMPU
COMMERCES
ACCESSIBLES

P Tulipe

Déviation
Porte de Namur
Naamse-poort
Flagey
P. Tulipe

Fietsers
afstappen

Déviation–Omleiding

Omleiding

Levi's
FOR WOMEN, MEN & KIDS
Monday to Saturday
DOCKERS
EXCEPTE LIVRAISONS
UITGEZONDERD
HOMMES
FEMMES

Solutions for appropriating areas in public spaces.

0484 881669
H

HITACHI
WANTY
Stabil
ARE YOU GOING ? LIVE HERE?
DEMOLITION DEMO J.V.
ZONE
P

FLANDERS GATE

January 2007

March 2008

April 2008

July 2008

September 2008

November 2009

December 2009

January 2010

April 2010

August 2010

September 2010

October 2012

June 2013

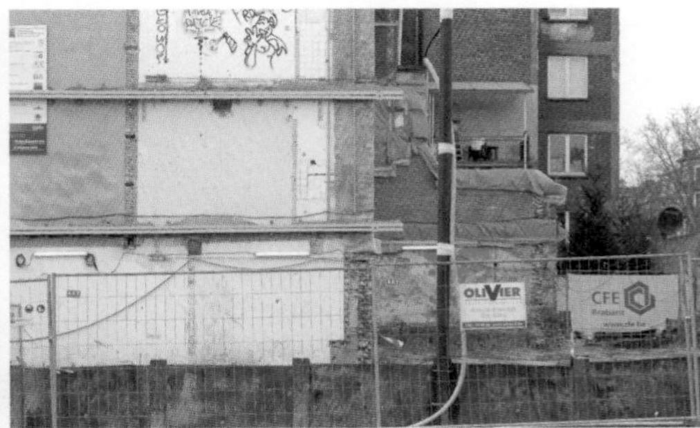

December 2013

May 2014

June 2017

Construction site Erasmushogeschool, Schootstraat (Brussels)

High voltage works, Koolmijnenkaai (Molenbeek)

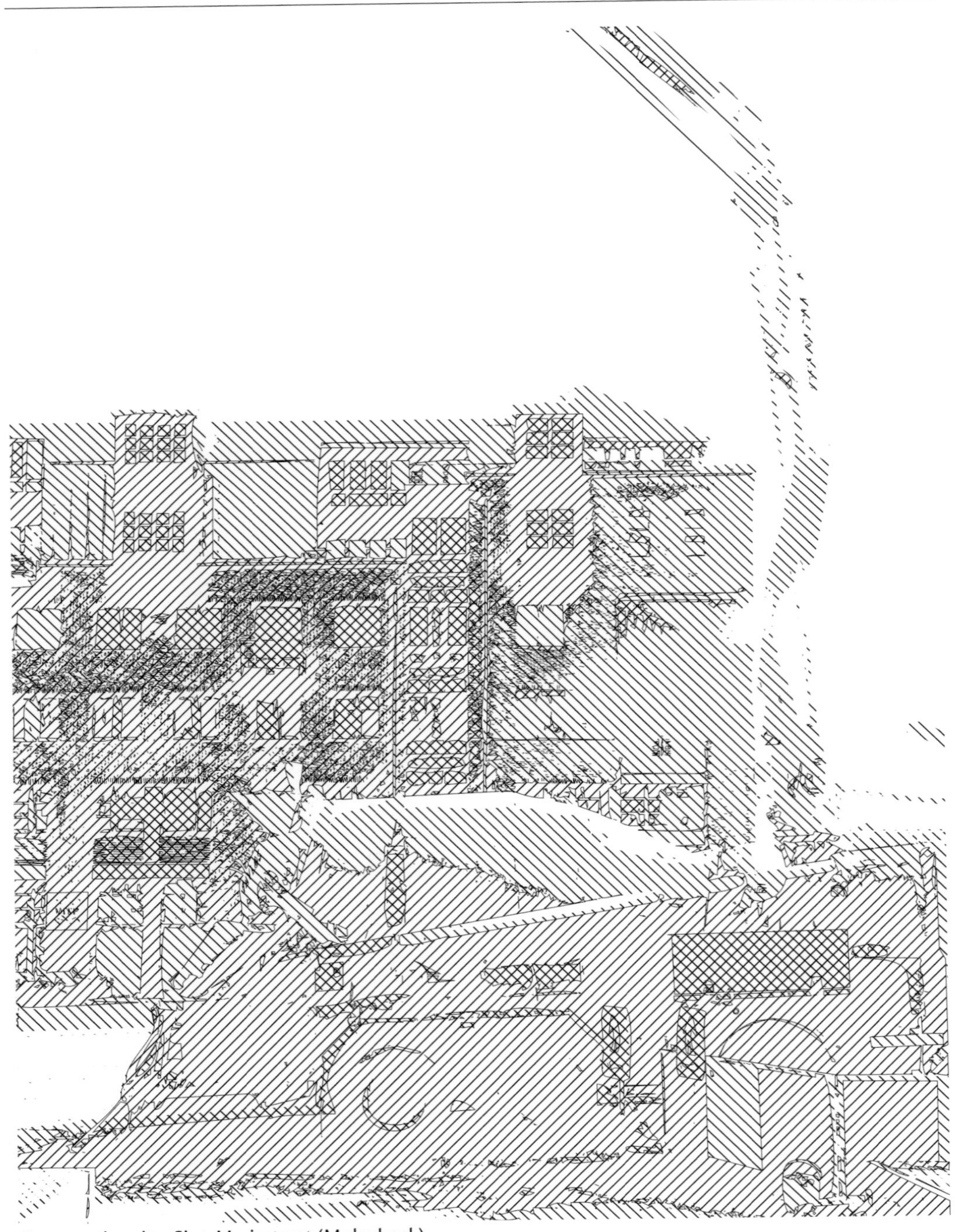

Construction site, Sint-Mariastraat (Molenbeek)

Construction site COOVI-CERIA car park, Bergensesteenweg (Anderlecht)

1000 BXL
BXL
1000
KMS
DAVID
1020
BOBOX
1030

1050
NIQUE
LA
POLICE
1050
XL
LACANCHE
BRU
LUX
1080
1050
1050
ARTI
1050·SOT
1080
1080 MOLEM
1210
1080
ON TA REPE
12
1210

Elin Herlaar

MOSAIC NEIGHBOURHOOD

Walking down my street I noticed these special mosaics and started photographing them. I discovered that they are the work of artist Ingrid Schreyers who started replacing the missing and broken cobbles with these colourful mosaics.

Erika Sprey

KINGS OF JEU DE BALLE

The *Jeu de Balle* square is world famous for its flea market. Local authorities tried to open up this institution for other types of markets and free the space of cars, but to no avail. The vendors' colourful diesel trucks amuse me, but they also annoy me, as they are noisy, stinky and behave like the incontestable kings of the square.

Letters on all kinds of supports and different situations intrigue me. When I see them in the streets, blown up to huge proportions, it seems to me like they have regained their initial form again. They are simple 'word images' again, just like I got to know them at first as a child, only in the shape of a different word, like 'garage' or 'café'. For this map I revealed the most beautiful ones in the Marolles. It's a reading of the city, my personal way of looking at this part of town – my type of Marolles.

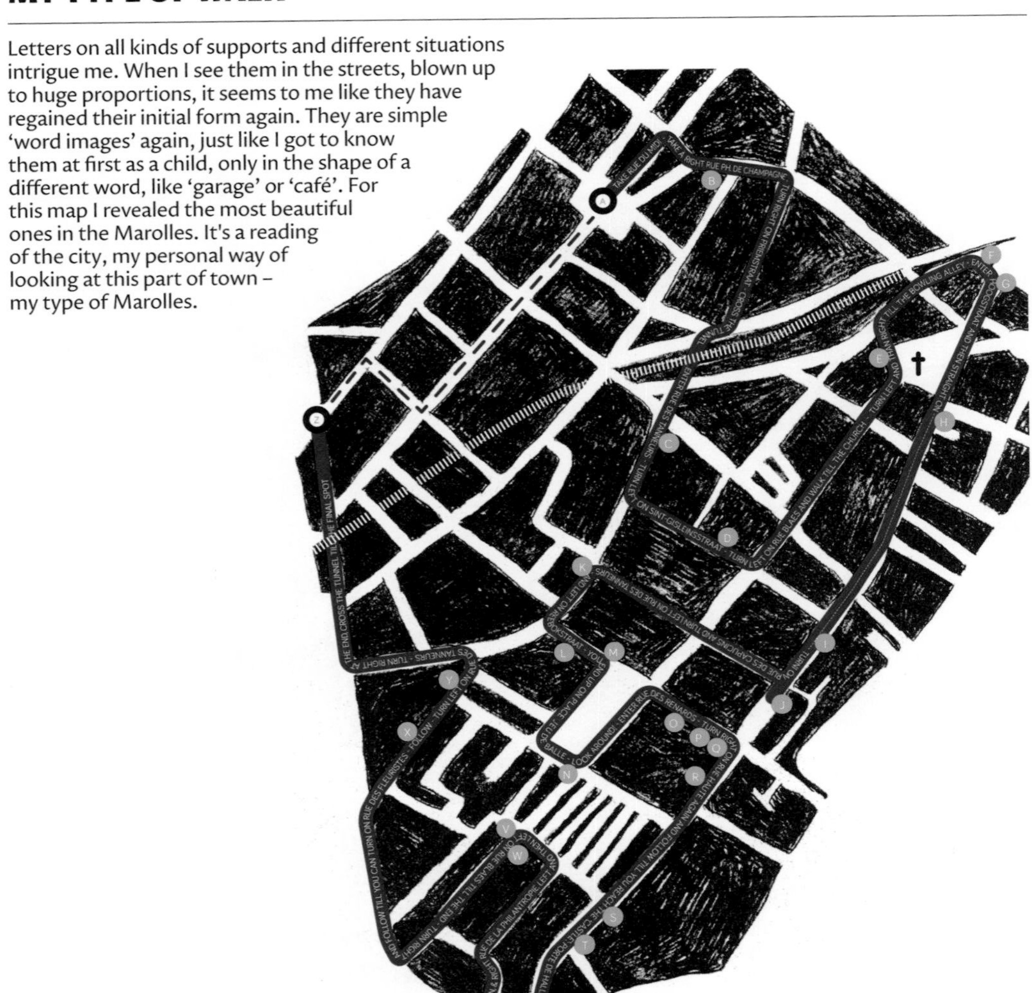

- A HOTEL A LA GRANDE CLOCHE
- B REPARATIONS DE CHAUSSURES RUE TERRE NEUVE
- C CITÉ MERCHE–PÊDE
- D KINDERTUIN
- E STEFANTIEK
- F SUPER BOWLING CROSLY
- G BIERES
- H AU BON JAVA
- I IMPASSE DE VARSOVIE WARSCHOUGANG
- J AUX CISEAUX D'OR
- K AUX FOYER
- L MAISON COOREMAN VOLAU LE GIBIER WILD GEVOGELTE POULETS A LA BROCHE
- M BAINS BADEN
- N IN DEN BLAUWEN LEMMEN
- O AUBERGE DU ROVENDAEL
- P 'T WERM WOETER HET WARM WATER L'EAU CHAUDE
- Q RENARD
- R BEURFIN
- S MUSEUM
- T SINT-PIETERSGASTHUIS
- U LE JAUCON
- V PALAIS DU PANTALON
- W TRIPERIE
- X CASA MARI 1974
- Y TOUT POUR LA PECHE
- Z PERLE 28 CAULIER

BAINS

Poulets a la Broche

MAISON COOREMAN
VOLAILLE GIBIER

AU BON JAVA

T'WERM WOETER HET WARM WATER L'EAU CHAUDE

M

BADEN

DE FLUITER

M
C
H
I
E
L
S

BRASSERIE
PLOEGMANS

CHAFF

AU
MOUTON
BLEU
IN DEN
BLAUWEN
LEMMEN

REPARATIONS
DE
CHAUSSURES
Rue
TERRE-NEUVE

CITÉ
MERCHIE-PÈDE

aux Ciseaux d'Or

MARCHÉ
BIO
BIO
MARKT

MUSEUM

Super
BOWLING
Crosly

STOPPAGE

LOUIS FRANSEN

L'ETOILE VERTE

Le Faucon

TRIPERIE

ALEX

BEURFIN

RESTAURANT

STEFANTIEK

L'IMAGINAIRE
Renard

TOUT POUR LA PECHE

KINDERTUIN

"AU FOYER"

HOPITAL
SAINT-PIERRE

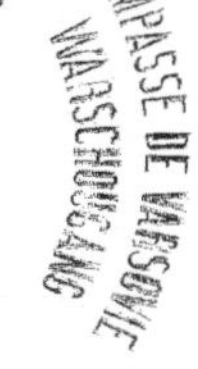

au bon
repos

CAULIER

A St MEDARD

In Schaarbeek I often visited hammam El Maghrab. Stepping into the humid, warm space felt like entering the womb of the city to enjoy long washing rituals together with friendly women and children. It took some time to discover there were more hammams in every district. Some were obvious with a lot of signs and flashy light boxes, others were hard to discover between the houses, only showing a little sign with 'Femmes, Hommes'.

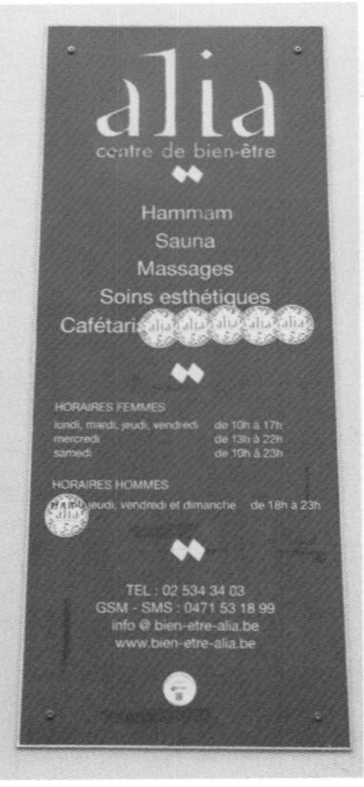

HAMMAM DU MIDI, Brussels

HAMMAM DU BONHEUR, Sint-Gillis

HAMMAN SALEM, Molenbeek

HAMMAN LA PACHA, Ganshoren

HAMMAN EL MAGHRAB, Schaarbeek

HAMMAN BILADI, Sint-Jans-Molenbeek

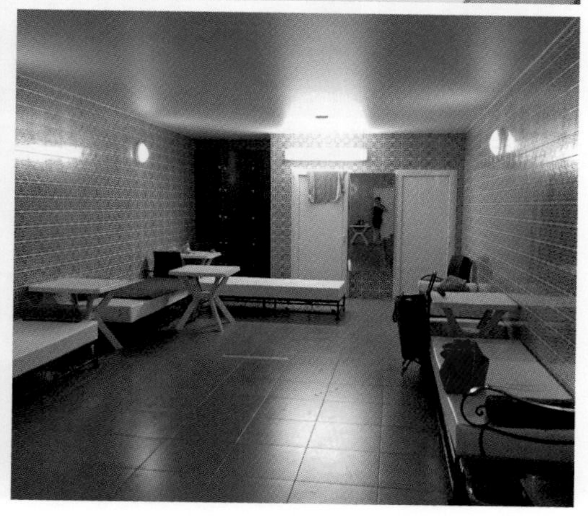

Selected doorhandels from housing block E. Tollenaerestraat, Laneusstraat, Richard Neyberglaan en Prudent Boslaan

2b
RESIDENCE

Ellen Helsen

CAT CLAN

Lost cats connect neighbours and neighbours make a neighbourhood. But we're facing the end of the growing vagabond cat population; birth control has been introduced because cats have to be sterilized since 2018. This means the end of the Brussels nomad cat clan existence. Nowadays, cat caretakers need official permission. Luckily there are still some hidden caretakers left, like Willy, who makes soft hay beds and cat breakfasts in his backyard. And there is the Dufour family who are kindly educating vagabonds to grow into decent and respectable, well-mannered house cats. I closely observed them after our cat Minou disappeared.

The location

Potential Escape routes

(A)
1. Through son Noam's open room window
2. On the roof along the garden wall between our house and our neighbours' house.
3. On through the neighbours' neighbours' house, visiting friends Léonor, Théo, Noa, Tina, Sacha, Léa and Lola on the way.
4. Balancing on a narrow wall to see her redhead friend with no name, the 'upholsterer's' cat. Sitting together on the wall, watching the moon.
5. On through the scary big dog's territory. teasing the scary big dog. trying not to fall into the scary big dog's garden.
6. Over the little roof of the back garden house, trying not to fall. Making her way to meet 'Scarface', the most virile neighbourhood cat. Falling hopelessly in love with Scarface, on the road, through the night, on through the abandoned houses.

(B) On to the terrace and into the branches of the (Christmas) oldest pine tree in the neighbourhood – born in 1972, aka 'HLM (*Habitation à loyer modéré*) des Pigeons', looking for a bird snack. Walking further, trying to cross Chaussée de Ninove. This will be a dead end.

Borders of Minou's territory

Dénouement

8.45pm, 03/06/2018
stifling heat, ±30°C
in heat
Minou disappeared

1.34 am, 04/06/2018
stifling
in heat, hungry, thirsty, still madly in love
Called Minou's name several times in the backyard, woke up 3 neighbours

06.34 am, 04/06/2018
Called her name several times in the backyard, woke up 2 neighbours and the red head cat.

9am–9pm, 04/06/2018
Looked for Minou the whole day. Rang all the neighbours' doorbells, combed out the territory of the 'Dichtkunst' cat clan.

9.40pm, 04/06/2018
Minou spotted by Willy. Neighbour Cat Catch Operation (NCCO) in Scrathy's garden. Minou defended by Scarface and finally caught by daughter Jaad.

05/06/2018
still stifling
tired and thirsty

Legende

- Wild cats
- Half-domesticated cat
- Domesticated cats
- Future and long-awaited cat
-  Cats with disabilities
-  Missing cats
- Black cats
- Cats in heat

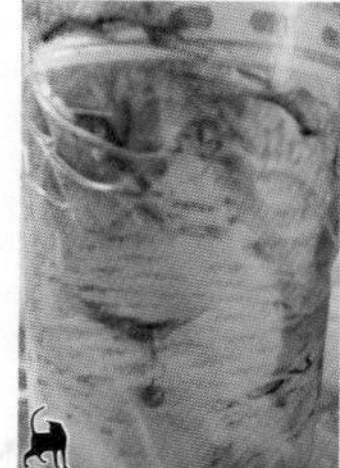

Misty

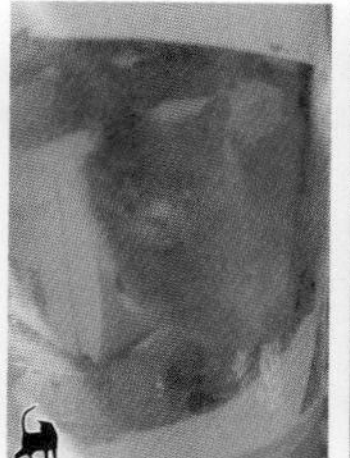

WI FI

Aiko

The Dichtkunst Cat Clan

Gaston Junior, *Pauline's house*

Lola, *Tina's kitten, triplet sister of Sacha and Léa, currently residing at the Dufours house*

Minou, *kid from domesticated cat and unknown father, very beautiful, very sexual*

Redhead battered face, **Scarface**

Scratchy, *multilingual Italian, English, French cat*

Theo, *found as a kitten in Madam Dufour's colleague's garden, currently living at the Dufour house*

3 Legged cat

Brown tiger

Black and white feet **Dandy,** *well-shaped moustache*

Dupond & Dupond, *white and black, black and white cat*

Hibiskus, *currently resides at Dichtkunstlaan, long grey haires. living with the psychologist at the Dichtkunstlaan*

Lea, *Tina's kitten, triplet sister of Lola ans Sacha, currently residing at the Dufours house*

Leonore, *found in a cardboard box, Chaussée de Ninove, occupies the 1st floor at the Dufour family's house*

Macha, *black cat found abandoned in a vegetable garden on a nearby waste ground , nowadays an allotment, adopted and and presently residing with the Stas family*

Noa, *found as a kitten in Julie's back garden*

Bonji, *the 'upholsterer's' cat Ninoofse Steenweg*

Sacha *with Lola & Léa, Tina's kitten. Triplet brother of Lola and Léa, currently residing at the Dufours house.*

Tina, *found pregnant at Rue van Soust, currently residing at the Dufour house*

Joud Toamah

OH, PSITTACINES!

In 1974 a group of 40 rose-ringed parakeets were set free by the owner of the Meli Zoo and Attraction Park near the Atomium who wanted to make Brussels more colourful. Now there are up to 10,000 green parakeets residing in Brussels alongside indigenous pigeons and woodpeckers. Some people welcome the birds as an

exotic delight, but others decry them as a dangerous invasive species. You can hear the parakeets in parks and if you look closely enough you can see them sitting up high in the trees, intermingling with the leaves.

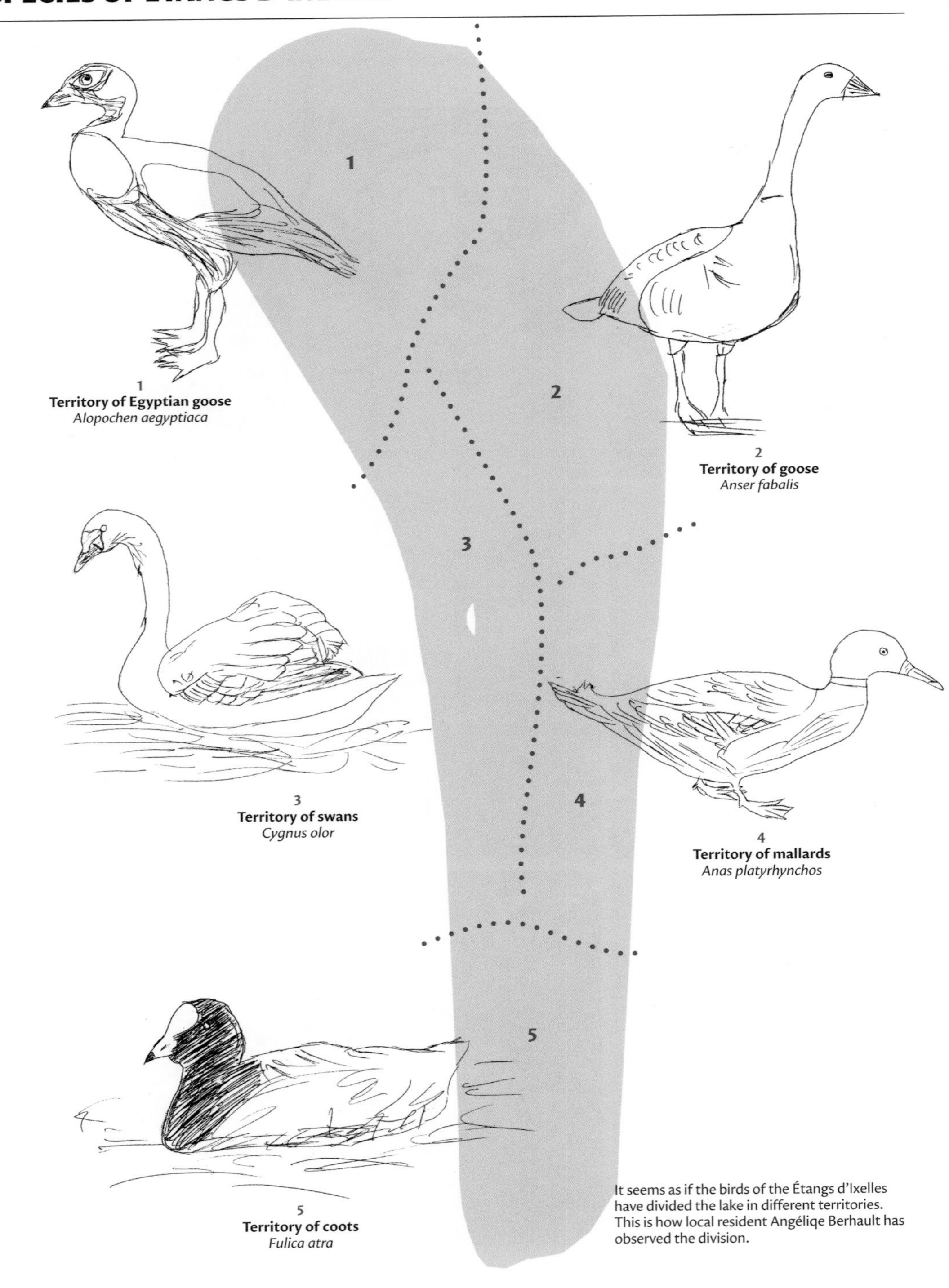

1
Territory of Egyptian goose
Alopochen aegyptiaca

2
Territory of goose
Anser fabalis

3
Territory of swans
Cygnus olor

4
Territory of mallards
Anas platyrhynchos

5
Territory of coots
Fulica atra

It seems as if the birds of the Étangs d'Ixelles have divided the lake in different territories. This is how local resident Angéliqe Berhault has observed the division.

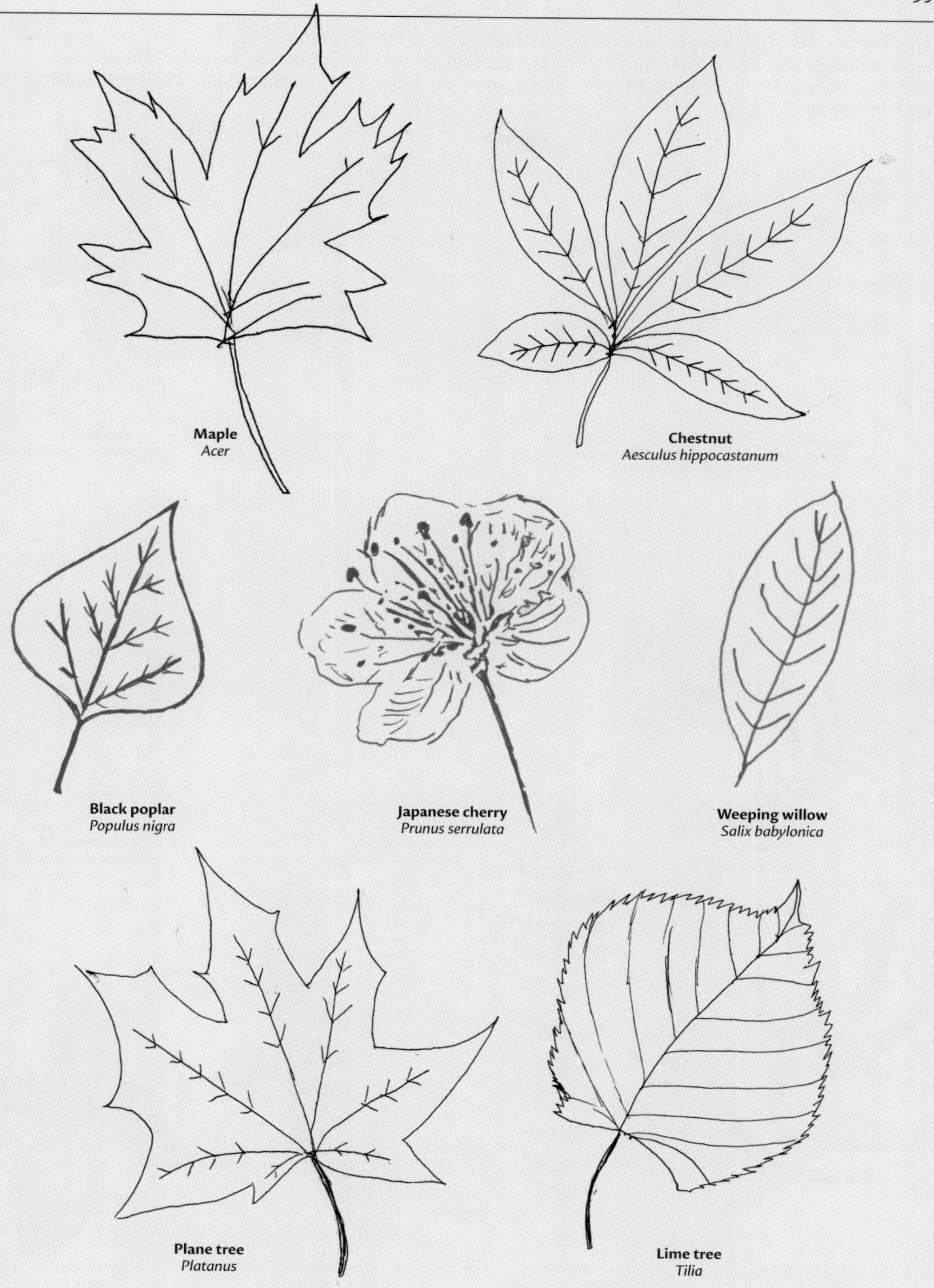

Maple
Acer

Chestnut
Aesculus hippocastanum

Black poplar
Populus nigra

Japanese cherry
Prunus serrulata

Weeping willow
Salix babylonica

Plane tree
Platanus

Lime tree
Tilia

ESSENTIAL GARDEN

These herbs of the public *Jardin Essentiel** in the *Duden Park* in Forest are primarily meant for making tea and extracts, to spice up and colour vinegars. The leading principle of the selection of the very diverse herbs is to maximize the experience in terms of taste, colour, smell and touch.These 'ordinary' species ultimately all prove to be very special.

Common Sage
Salvia officinalis

Marjoram
Origanum majorana

Thyme
Thymus vulgaris

Rosemary
Rosmarinus officinalis

Tansy
Tanacetum vulgare

Absinthium
Artemisia absinthium

Southernwood
Artemisia abrotanum

Lemon Verbena
Aloysia triphylla

Yarrow
Achillea millefolium

Lemon Balm
Melissa officinalis

Mint
Mentha sp.

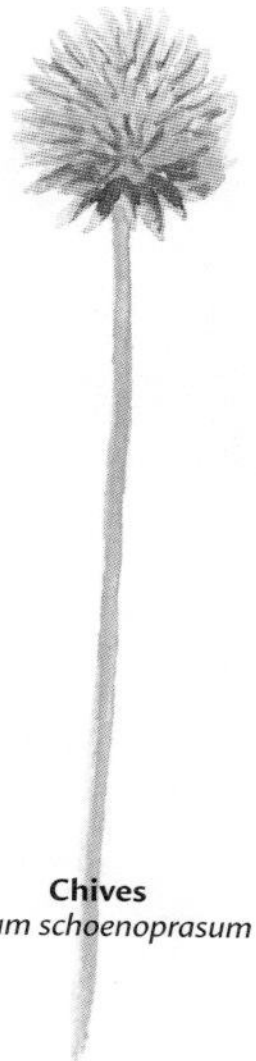

Chives
Allium schoenoprasum

Lavender
Lavandula angustifolium

Savory
Satureja hortensis

Immortelle d'Italie
Helychrysum Italicum

Fennel
Foeniculum vulgare

Brassica Nigra
Brassica nigra

Chamomile
Chamaemelum nobile

Calendula
Calendula Officinalis

Opium Poppy
Papaver somniferum

Indian Cress
Tropaeolum majus

* 'Jardin Essentiel' is an artwork by Rudy J. Luijters and was developed within the framework of the international festival Parckdesign 2016. Ever since it has been in use as a community garden.

I have been living in Molenbeek for the past seven years, during which time the neighbourhood has continued to struggle against stigmatization. Despite the existing problems and challenges, there are many aspects and initiatives from within the community that are not recognized and many voices not taken into account, making Molenbeek an ever-changing, diverse and inspiring municipality of Brussels.

Potager la rue

Majorelle

With Molenbeek being a rather densely populated urban area, the hidden green capsules of community gardens are places to retreat from city life and to experience the diverse community of Molenbeek while digging, planting, composting and sharing cups of freshly harvested mint tea.

Scheutbos

L'ambition

Francesca Chiacchio

LAST RAYS OF SUNSHINE

These are the best places in Brussels to enjoy the last of the day's sunshine.

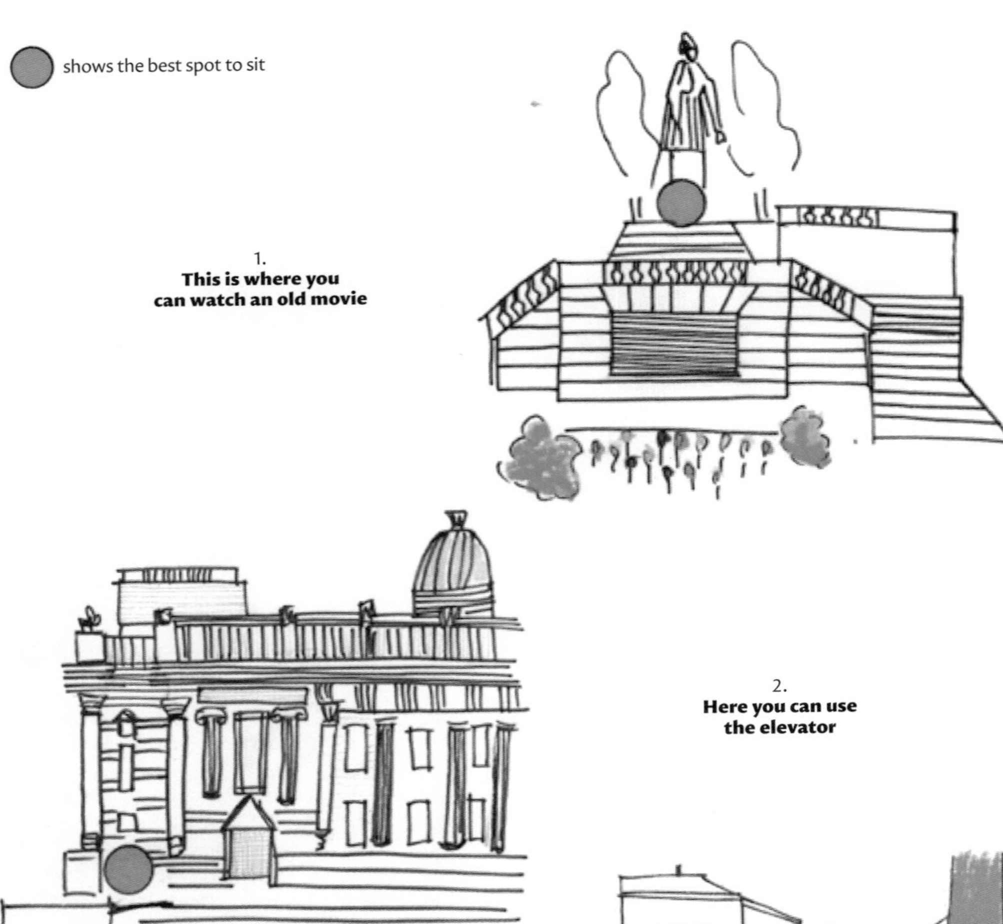

3.
Nearby travelling pigeons are celebrated and where the Ferris wheel appears in wintertime

4.
It is in a park,
1190 is the code,
and there is sand

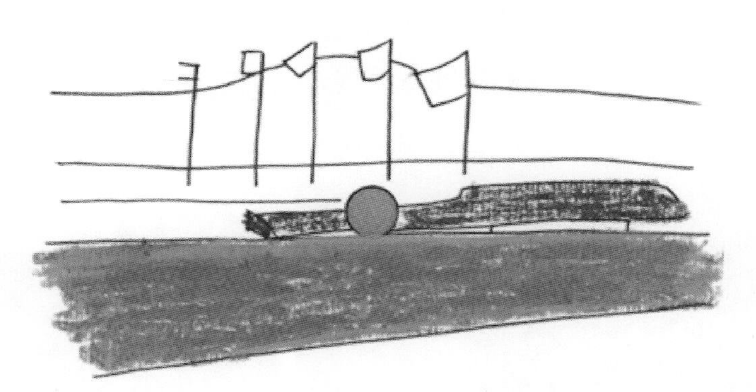

5.
It is known by those
who love rowing

6.
It is a square
that has to do with aviation

King, queen and four children

Royal Domain of Laeken
1 860 000 m²
Open to the royal family 24/24

Open to the public
21 days/year
9.30am–5.30pm

source: www.environnement.brussels

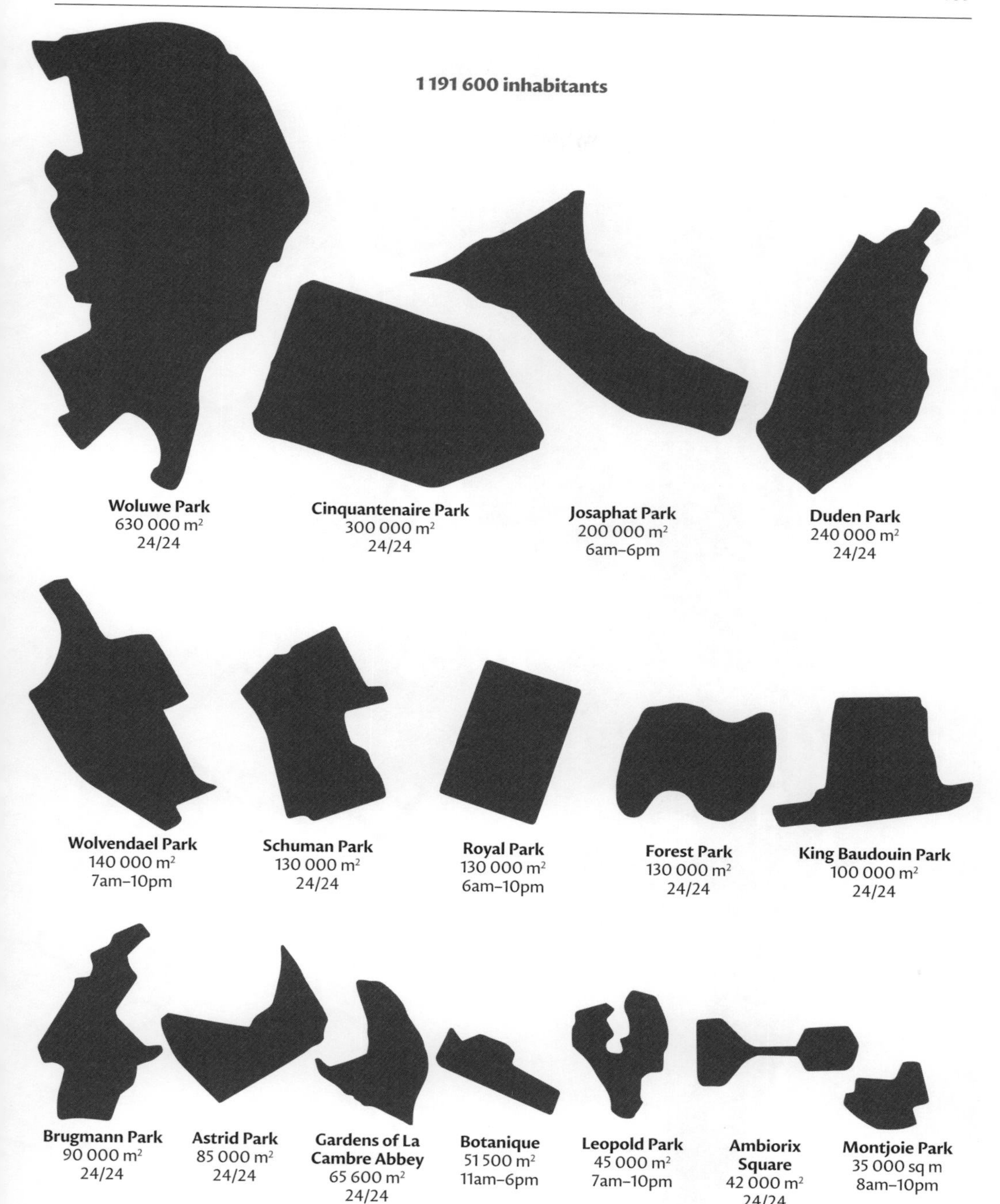
1 191 600 inhabitants
Woluwe Park
630 000 m²
24/24
Cinquantenaire Park
300 000 m²
24/24
Josaphat Park
200 000 m²
6am–6pm
Duden Park
240 000 m²
24/24
Wolvendael Park
140 000 m²
7am–10pm
Schuman Park
130 000 m²
24/24
Royal Park
130 000 m²
6am–10pm
Forest Park
130 000 m²
24/24
King Baudouin Park
100 000 m²
24/24
Brugmann Park
90 000 m²
24/24
Astrid Park
85 000 m²
24/24
Gardens of La Cambre Abbey
65 600 m²
24/24
Botanique
51 500 m²
11am–6pm
Leopold Park
45 000 m²
7am–10pm
Ambiorix Square
42 000 m²
24/24
Montjoie Park
35 000 sq m
8am–10pm

King Baudouin Foundation Leopold Park, priority interventions, Marco Schmitt, January 2009, summary of land properties

Friche Eggevoort is an urban wasteland in the heart of the European Quarter, at stake for everyone, to be taken by anyone.

This 'friche' linked many stakeholders and even more agendas: water, art, gardening, commons, governance, public space, biodiversity, heritage, urbanism, meeting space, science and experiment. It was addressed by the communes, the Capital Region, the Federal State, the EU Parliament, research, lobby and cultural institutions, neighbourhood committees and associations, local residents.

Its undefinedness invited all kinds of uses. A free zone and platform for discussion and experiment came into being. Are those unregulated places the right space to learn to collaborate, co-create, co-decide?

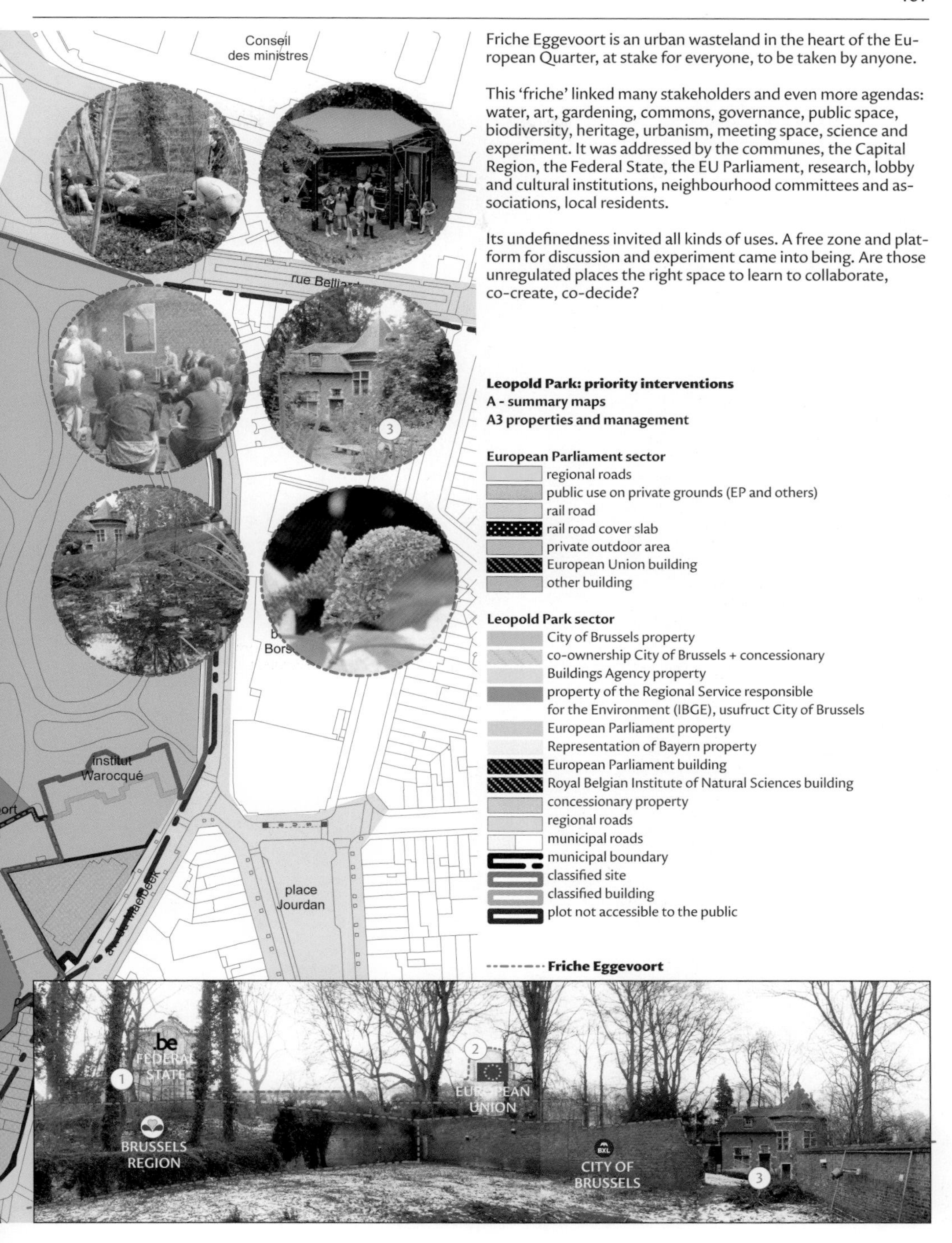

Leopold Park: priority interventions
A - summary maps
A3 properties and management

European Parliament sector

- regional roads
- public use on private grounds (EP and others)
- rail road
- rail road cover slab
- private outdoor area
- European Union building
- other building

Leopold Park sector

- City of Brussels property
- co-ownership City of Brussels + concessionary
- Buildings Agency property
- property of the Regional Service responsible for the Environment (IBGE), usufruct City of Brussels
- European Parliament property
- Representation of Bayern property
- European Parliament building
- Royal Belgian Institute of Natural Sciences building
- concessionary property
- regional roads
- municipal roads
- municipal boundary
- classified site
- classified building
- plot not accessible to the public

Friche Eggevoort

Due to a lack of public playgrounds for young people, alternative places are used to hang out and to imagine other realities. For the youth in Molenbeek the West Station offers many grey zones for their fantasies.

Railway tracks of Beekkant

Park around the railway tracks of Beekkant

West Station bridge

Down the bridge of the West Station

Images from storyboard film 'Rosie and Maussa', Dorothé van Den Berghe 2018

Shilemeza Prins touching **Statue of Everard't Serclaes,** Grand Place, *Julien Dillens 1902*

Brussel is wat niemand soms verwacht, klein geluk en veel genieten. Met een beeld van een stervende legende die geluk schenkt. Wrijf je over zijn gelaat dan krijg je zowaar een Ketje. "Vra is vry en weier is daarby."

Menneken Pis, Stoofstraat * Eikstraat, *Jerome Duquesnoy 1619*

Een stad zo vriendelijk, een stad gebouwd op vijf hoekstenen en dit zorgt ervoor dat het gezin dat hier leeft zo bijzonder is, dat de hele wereld zich thuis voelt. Onze held en sterkte Manneken Pis. En in die geest van traditie en kunst, leren we de troeven van onze stad en zo kunnen we dit dagelijks delen met de wereld in een ceremonie; Brussel is Manneke Pis.

Bruegel at work, église Notre-Dame de la Chapelle, *Tom Frantzen, 2015*

Brussel is een waarde zonder zwaard. Met kwast en penseel en een mooi uitzicht worden dingen dus reëel, wat een tafereel. Als je dan nog twijfelt of weifelt, Pieter Breugel. Brussel is thuis.

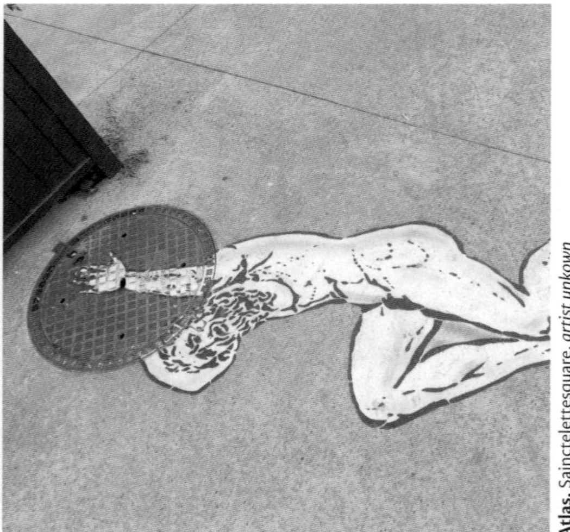

Atlas, Sainctelettesquare, *artist unkown*

Vijfhoeken, vijf sculpturen, een stad zonder muren aan het water en wie gluren? De buren. Brussel is... een gezin met een braal van talen met beelden en sculpturen, bruisende klanken, en een mengelmoes van mensen en dié mensen worden alleen maar gezien in het licht van 'n andere mens. "Ubuntu"

Madame Chapeau, Zuidstraat, *Tom Frantzen, 2000*

"En het is alweer, aan het weer, geen keer... De zomer is de kluts kwijt" En niemand valt te verwijten. Niet een wispelturige vrouw. Dit is Madam Chapeau en straks zal dit nog regenen. "Ateriën gauget nog regenen." Wat gepast, gezellig en solidair, want wat is een vrouw zonder haar sjakos? Salam a laikum. سلام عليكم

De Vaartkapoen, Sainctelettesquare, *Tom Frantzen, 1985*

Bruxelloïs. Dit gezin dat soms worstelt met de dagdagelijkse rompslomp, en dan nog strompelt, een voortvluchtige uit de stinkende, maar veilige riolen. Waar dat het krioelt van het onmisbare zwarte goud Bienvenue à...

Het Zinneke, Rue des Chartreux, *Tom Frantzen, 2000*

Brussel is... een stad die dicht met gezichten, met het mengen van culturen en sculpturen. Een zinnenstad met haar pissende zinnekes maken pissende reacties los. Daarvan ligt niemand wakker, en daarvoor wordt niemand veracht. Ça va nog.

Jaques Brel, Oud Korenhuis, *Tom Frantzen, 2017*

Een stem. De inhoud is herkenbaar en tijdloos. Zijn krachtige stem laat de velden en bomen roerloos staan, omdat wat volgt komt uit het diepste van een mensenhart. Een vrolijkheid of een droefheid in zijn stem die de andersheid van de mens in mij en andere mensen raakt. Het geluid brengt mensen bij mekaar, en emoties versmelten in een draaikolk van dagdagelijkse geluiden, melodieën die herkenbaar zijn, in het bijzijn van andere mensen. Want kijk er langs, en dan lijkt de wereld anders, en zo worden de verlangens dragelijk.

Augustin Daniel Comte Belliard
Koningstraat / Rue Royale

Jean-Jacques-Edouard Chapelié
Militaire School / Ecole Militaire

Le Palmier ou Le Martyr
Kruidtuin / Jardin Botanique

Fontaine Nicolas-Jean Rouppe
Rouppeplein / Place Rouppe

Charles Rogier
Vrijheidsplein / Place de la Liberté

Charles Lorraine
Museumplein / Place du Musée

David
Sint-Jacob-op-Koudenberg-kerk / Eglise Saint-Jacques-sur-Coudenberg

Narcisse
Warandepark / Parc de Bruxelles

Samson lançant des renards dans les Champs de Philistins
Jubelpark / Le Parc du Cinquantenaire

Antoine Wiertz
Raymond Blyckaertsplein /
Place Raymond Blyckaerts

L'Esclave repris par les chiens
Ter Kamerenbos / Bois de la Cambre

Les quatre âges
Kruidtuin / Jardin Botanique

La Charité
Warandepark / Parc de Bruxelles

Bernard Van Orley
Kleine Zavel / Petit Sablon

Le Dompteur de chevaux
Louizalaan / Avenue Louise

La Surprise
Paleis der Academiën
Palais des Académies

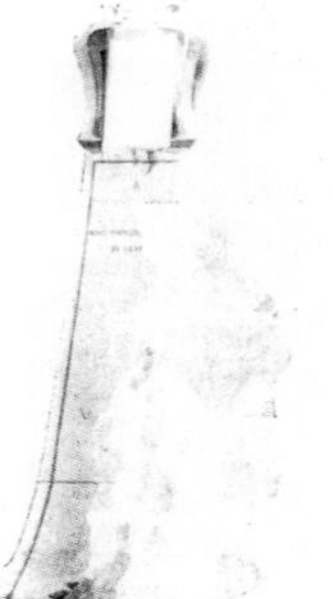

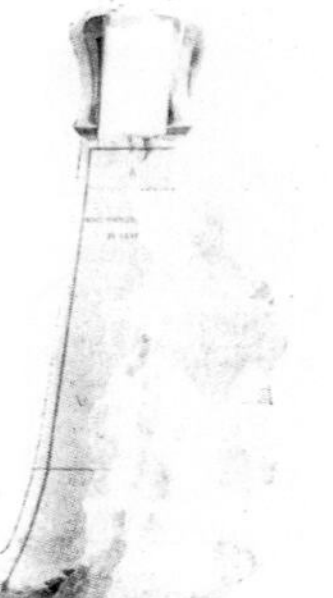

Frédéric de Merode
Martelarenplein / Place des Martyrs

L'Art allemand
Paleis voor Schone Kunsten /
Palais des Beaux-Arts

Original photos of 'Les Sculptures de Plein Air à Bruxelles' of Pol. Meirsschaut, printed and edited by Emile Bruylant, 1900.

The walls of Brussels breathe and speak, but do not lie. For they are formed by layers of imbricated strata where all epochs survive and pile up, intact but still trembling and mutually interacting. Beneath the flat and seemingly immobile surface of the present walls of our cherished capital, opaque and stubborn histories survive and move with the rhythm of the everyday, leaving indelible traces on the consciousness of its passers-by.

Koloniënstraat, Brussels city centre

Bust of Leopold II, Duden Park, Vorst

Congo monument, Jubelpark

Edmond Thieffry statue, Etterbeek, intersection Boileaulaan, Mesenslaan

Previously the **Fondation de la Couronne of the Independent State of Congo,** Koningsplein, back of the Belvue Museum

Brederodestraat, **former headquarters of the Congo Free State**

Equestrian statue of Leopold II, Troonplein, Brussels

Congo monument, Jubelpark

Futur Place Lumumba, Elsene, Sint-Bonifatius

Equestrian statue of Leopold II, Troonplein, Brussels

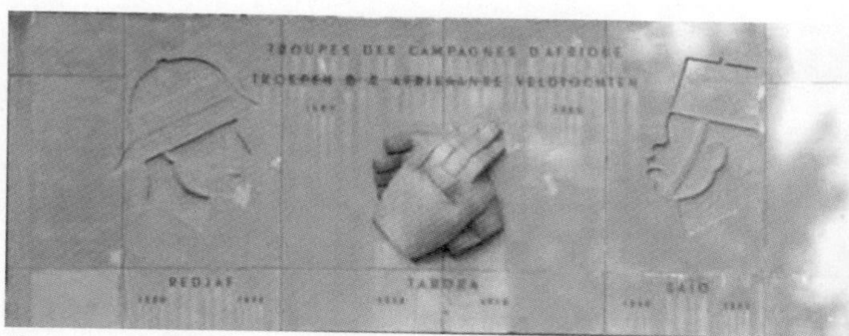

Monument to the African campaigns, Helmet, Schaarbeek

Aux Etterbeekois, pioniers de la civilisation morts au Congo, Etterbeek, Louis Hapstraat on façade near Sint-Pietersplein

Au delà de l'espoir, **Statue of Freddy Simba**, Matonge, Elsene

Tarvo Varres

UNAVAILABLE MEMORY (THE CORNERS OF BRUSSELS)

Corners of Brussels are shot off main streets, behind major buildings and institutions. Details in architecture point to the history of this complex and grand European city; while subtle little clues, marks, signs, graffiti and such suggest multiple narratives, possible scenarios, hint at the people who have been there or are yet to come.

In this angle, most buildings look alike, free of their ego or ideology. Notions of contingency and vulnerability emerge in these continuous situations of uncertainty, of multiple options and choices, in personal vertical time. Do we know what exactly guides us in our decisions?

Most people know about *Liberté, Égalité, Fraternité* on the French flag, but few seem to know Belgium has its foundations engraved in the heart of Brussels. The Congress column refers to the predecessor of the current Parliament, which was established in November 1830, immediately after the Belgian Revolution. This was the body that approved the Belgian Constitution in February 1831. In Europe at the time, this Constitution was revolutionary, for it gave the Belgian population four main freedoms neighbouring populations didn't have yet: freedom of religion, freedom of association, freedom in education and freedom of the press. The nearby *Place de la Liberté* (Liberty Square) has four roads leading off its square: *Rue de la Presse, Rue de l'Enseignement, Rue de l'Association* and *Rue des Cultes*. If we go further, many of the adjoining streets also have names reminiscent of the birth of Belgium: *rue de la Révolution, rue du Gouvernement provisoire* and *Place des Barricades*.

PLACE DE LA LIBERTÉ
VRIJHEIDSPLAATS
RUE DE
L'ASSOCIATION
BONDSTRAAT

RUE DE LA PRESSE
DRUKPERSSTRAAT

RUE DE L'ENSEIGNEMENT
ONDERWIJSSTRAAT

RUE DES
CULTES
EREDIENST
STRAAT

GOUVERNEMENT PROVISOIRE

For two months I walked around the Scheut neighbourhood (Anderlecht) and presented the sentence 'I am who I am becoming' to passers-by, asking what this meant to them and how they would translate it in their language.

Ik ben wie ik word
Nederlands (België) — néerlandais (Belgique)

Je suis qui je deviens
Frans (België) — français (Belgique)

این منم که تغییر می کنم.
Dari (Farsi) (Afghanistan) — dari (farsi) (Afghanistan)

Аз съм тази, в която ще се превърна
Bulgaars (Bulgarije) — bulgare (Bulgarie)

我将成为我自己
Chinees (Mandarijn)(China) — chinois (mandarin) (Chine)

Nazali oyo nalingi nazala
Lingala (Congo) — lingala (RD Congo)

Ich bin wer ich werde
Duits (Duitsland) — allemand (Allemagne)

Soy aquél en quien me convertiré
Spaans (Ecuador) — espagnol (Equateur)

Είμαι αυτός που γίνομαι
Grieks (Griekenland) — grec (Grèce)

Nipi nitakavyo
Swahili (Uganda/Rwanda) — swahili (Uganda/Rwanda)

Я є тим, ким я є
Oekraïens (Oekraïne) — ukrainien (Ukraine)

Tôi sẽ trở thành con người mà tôi muốn
Vietnamees (Vietnam) — vietnamien (Vietnam)

Ndi uwo ndiwe uko bukeye
Kirundi (Burundi) — kirundi (Burundi)

Eni ti mo fe je ni mo je
Yoruba (Nigeria) — yoruba (Nigéria)

Ko hande kala ebhanta diango mun
Peul (Guinee) — peul (Guinée)

Nipi nitakavyo
Swahili (Uganda/Rwanda) — swahili (Uganda/Rwanda)

Я є тим, ким я є
Oekraïens (Oekraïne) — ukrainien (Ukraine)

मैं हूँ जो मैं बनना चाहता हूँ
Hindi (Indië) — hindi (Inde)

Punjabi (Indië) **ਮੈਂ ਉਹ ਹਾਂ, ਜੋ ਮੈਂ ਬਣ ਰਿਹਾ ਹਾਂ** punjabi (Inde)

Urdu (Indië / Pakistan) **میں وہ ہوں جو بنوں گا** urdu (Inde / Pakistan)

Italiaans (Italië) **Sono colui che divento** italien (Italie)

Bamiléké (Kameroen) **Me beu ha' ze a nsi beu lah** bamiléké (Cameroun)

Kroatisch (Kroatië) **Ja sam onaj koji postajem** croate (Croatie)

Albanees (Albanië/Macedonië) **Unë jam çfarë jam duke u bërë** albanais (Albanie/Macédonie)

Arabisch (Marokko) **أنا سأكون ما أريد أن أصبح** arabe (Maroc)

Haussa (Kameroen/Niger) **Ina nan yanda zan zama** haoussa (Cameroun/Niger)

Pools (Polen) **Jestem tym, kim się staję** polonais (Pologne)

Eu sou aquilo no que estou a transformar-me
Portugees (Portugal) portugais (Portugal)

Roemeens (Roemenië/Moldavië) **Eu sunt cine am devenit** roumain (Roumanie/Moldavie)

Kinyarwanda (Rwanda) **Ndi uwo mba buri munsi** kinyarwanda (Rwanda)

Wolof (Senegal) **Man dana nek lu ma warra nek** wolof (Sénégal)

Aniga waxaan ahay qofka aan noqon doono
Somali (Somalië) somalien (Somalie)

Tajik (Tajikistan) **ИН МАНАМ КИ ИВАЗ МЕШАВАМ** tajik (Tajikistan)

བདག་ཉིད་བདག་གི་མགོན་ཡིན་ལ། །བདག་ཉིད་བདག་གི་དགྲ་ཡང་ཡིན། །ལེགས་དང་ཉེས་པ་བྱས་པ་ལ། །བདག་ཉིད་བདག་གི་དཔང་པོ་ཡིན།།
Lhasa Tibetaans (Tibet) tibétain (lhasa) (Tibet)

Gambaye (Tsjaad) **Man mto déou g maré** gambaye (Tchad)

Turks (Turkije) **Ben dönüşmekte olduğum kişiyim** turc (Turquie)

These banners were originally presented on 6 m-wide banners that decorated one of the large avenues of Scheut for several months.

Brussels is the political capital of the Brussels-Capital Region, Flanders, Belgium and the EU. It has several parliaments and governments, and hosts NATO on its territory. Most international organizations, NGOs and companies have a branch here and it is one of the cities with the most press correspondents and lobbyists in the world. This results in Brussels being the centre of an endless democratic buzz. The Civil society plays a prominent role in the democratic processes, with demonstrations, occupations and protests. Everyday there is one or other democratic action taking place in the streets and on the squares of Brussels. Join the movement!

Filter Cafe Filtre

Sainctelette square

Filter Cafe Filtre

Basisschool Kakelbont, Laken

Annelys de Vet

Karmelietenstraat

Margrit Coppé

Helihavenlaan / Boudewijnlaan

Schuman Square

Jean Rey Square

Margrit Coppé

Helihavenlaan / Boudewijnlaan

Rachida El Garani

Kruidtuinlaan

Montoyerstraat

Schuman Square

Cecile Harni

Municipality square, Molenbeek

Erika Sprey

Flagey Square

Cecile Harni

Maximiliaanpark

Cecile Harni

Nord station

Cecile Harni

Central Station

Sophie Feyder

PLACES OF HOPE

These are the places in Brussels that give me hope for a more breathable city in the future. In the strict environmental sense, but also in terms of the ability to live well collectively, resisting the pressures of a system that tries to convince us that we are in competition with one another for ever shrinking resources. Hence my mapping includes different citizen initiatives that I have encountered in my daily life and which inspire me for addressing several issues at once. I've added *joie de vivre* as a cause to defend, because without that there is nothing worth fighting for.

Marché des Tanneurs *Marolles*

The best organic market in town, situated in the popular neighbourhood 'les Marolles'. Their fair prices mean that they are paving the way towards making organic food more affordable to people of colour, including people from the neighbourhood. Everything is sold in bulk, greatly reducing packaging.

La Vieille Chéchette *St Gilles*

Cooperative café and bookshop. It's how you'd want the rest of the world to be: open, friendly, multi-generational, relaxed and with great books. Their way into the neighbourhood is via the kids, who love to hang out there.

Cinema Nova *Centre*

A real cultural institution of Brussels, an independent cinema mainly run by volunteers and absolute cinema freaks. In the summer, they organize outdoor projections in different parts of Brussels with the aim of bringing people to lesser known parts of the city and have a critical discussion on gentrification.

La Petite Epicerie *St Gilles*

Three Tunisian brothers run this tiny organic shop in the more working-class part of St Gilles. They hope to make the organic food movement more inclusive, going out of their way to make sure that everyone feels welcome to step into their shop.

Le Space *Quartier Dansaert*

Ex-fashion shop converted into activist café hosting all kinds of events representing an impressive range of political causes. As a result, one of the few places where convergence of struggles and intersectionality are actually taking place.

Globe Aroma *Centre*

Globa Aroma is an arts centre where refugee artists and undocumented artists are welcomed and get to meet local artists. In February 2018, 20 officers raided the centre and arrested 7 newcomer-artists. The " #Onevoicemany-alarms" campaign emerged in protest against this attack.

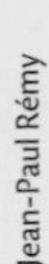

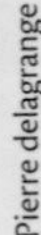

Symbols of causes

- environment
- feminism
- social exclusion
- queer
- urban mobility
- strengthening local life
- critical thought
- international solidarity
- racial inequality and decolonisation
- *joie de vivre*

Brasserie de la Senne *Molenbeek*

Local brewery priding itself for being 100% *bruxellois*. They make excellent beer using local products in a sustainable way. Plus they have really funky labels. They occasionally make a special edition to fund-raise for a particular political cause, such as the Potato Freedom Fighters.

Place Lumumba *Porte de Namur*

Place de Namur is the doorstep to the bustling Congolese neighbourhood Matonge. Part of the square situated there will be renamed 'Place Lumumba', after Patrice Lumumba. This decision followed years of ongoing mobilization of various associations calling to decolonize public space in the city.

Critical Mass *Porte de Namur*

Place de Namur is also the starting point of Critical Mass, a monthly gathering (every last Friday of the month, at 18.00) of bikers who stroll through Brussels *en masse*, to claim in a festive way their due space in the streets.

Plateforme Citoyenne de Soutien aux Réfugiés *North station*

One cold rainy night in January earlier this year, about 3000 citizens arrived at the Maximilien Park to form a human chain in protest against the police raids targeting refugees. They succeeded in blocking the police operation planned for that night.It is the daily meeting point for Brussels residents who wish to offer their home to refugees for the night.

Douche FLUX *Anderlecht*

Amazing idea of making showers and washing machines available to homeless people.Having the means to remain clean is crucial to maintaining one's dignity and is the precondition to any long-term social inclusion project.

#We too *Centre*

Brussels is internationally known for its contemporary dance scene, attracting dancers from all over the world. In the wake of the #MeToo campaign, female dancers started denouncing sexual abuse in their field under #WeToo. It is now a movement of 600 members and a bi-monthly meeting to plan out the feminist revolution in the performance world.

Jente Somers

Frédéric Moreau de Bellaing

All concerts I attended my first months in Brussels.

20-25 June 2017
LA CHEMINEE
Festival Mondial du Film Sauvage
Manuel J grotesque, Antoine Garrec

25 June 2017
NGHE
Soirée Nicey Music
Santé Loisirs présente: Banny Groove, pont à mousson, Eric Kinny

13 October 2017
NO SUPPLIES
Aposiopese présente : Taku Sugimoto Léo Dupleix Minami Saeki, Unfulfilleduo, Adjani

21 October 2017
ATELIERS CLAUS
Les Filles de Illighadad
Ifriqiyya Electrique, Gernas

24 October 2017
NIKO MATCHA
La Honte, Jean Marie Mercimek

29 October 2017
KUMIKO
Gayhaze : Josh cheon, Reza athar, Bora Bora, Gay haze djs aka Vieira-FLB-Disconsole

31 October 2017
LA ZINZINERIE
Monsters' Party
Von Wolf, Rough Ride, Hot Waves, Hard Fall Heart, Amour, The Retarded Rats

10 - 12 November 2017
BEURSSCHOUWBURG
festival schiev *ELG, Black Zone Myth Chant, Machine Woman, Mr. Mitch, N.M.O, Hiele / Clara !*

25 November 2017
NIKO MATCHA
Pont à Mousson, Loto Retina, Me-And

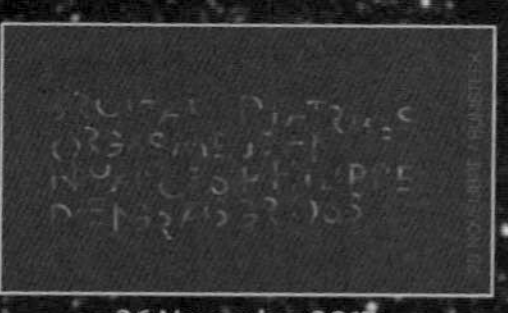

26 November 2017
RUMSTEEK
JeanPhilippeGross, Diatribes, BruitalOrgasme, NuancesDengrais

02 December 2017
NIKO MATCHA
Charlène Darling-Céline et Jean François

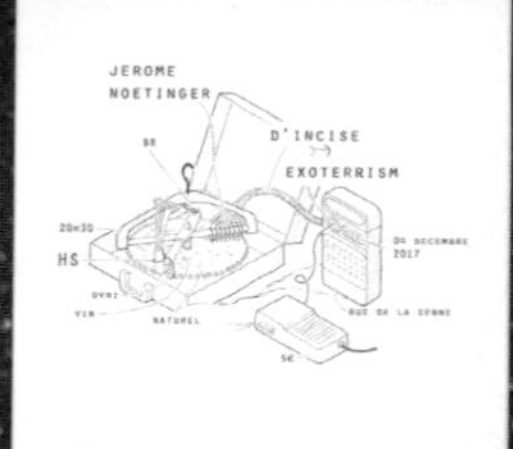

04 December 2017
HS63
Jerome Noetinger, D'incise, Exoterrism

09 December 2017
BARLOK
Jezu Makes NOISE #3
Krakenizer, Dani Cosmic, the Bipolar Nico Dovan, Amour, Illuminatek

12 December 2017
ATELIER 210
Blackout Session #61
Miles Davis - In a Silent Way (1969)

17 December 2017
NIKO MATCHA
Rouge Gorge, Dance Divine

13 January 2018
KUMIKO
Nose Job W Rick Shiver DJ Sundae

17 January 2018
HS63
Jean Colin, Le Renard

19 January 2018
Q-02
The Third Guy, Simon Bolay - Yannick Guédon

29 January 2018
HS63
Thomas Tilly , Fred Alstadt , J.P. De Gheest

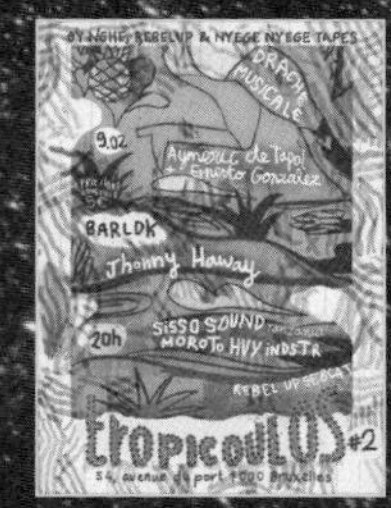

09 February 2018
BARLOCK
Tropicoulos 2: Nyege Nyege Tapes, Johnny Haway, Rebel Up & more

02 February 2018
BUREAU DE L'ETOILE
Fiesta En El Vagio
Aymeric de Tapol, Carrageenan, Project local inutile, DJ Bien Lati

09 February 2018
MADAME MOUSTACHE
Jessica93 Usé

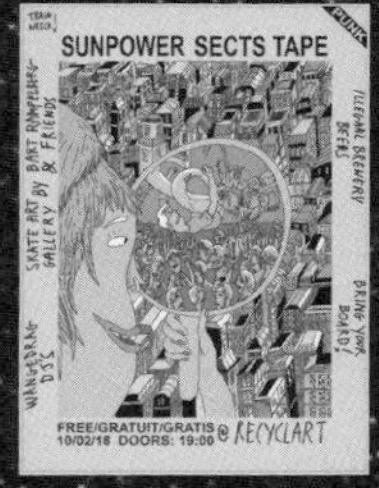

10 February 2018
RECYCLART
Trainwreck, SECTS TAPE, Sunpowe, Wanderdrag

11 February 2018
BRASSERIE ATLAS
Cantenac Dagar, Nah, Les Maitres Fous

19 February 2018
HS63
Gianfranco Piombo, Le Jour Du Seigneur, Michel Henritzi

21 February 2018
BARLOCK
TG Gondard
Tôle Froide, Henchman

05 March 2018
BARLOK
Faîne Soldat Exoterrism Culture émotion

09 March 2018
LE LAC
Concert de Musique Protocolaire #2 Fred Deltendre

10 March 2018
LA VALLEE
2files 4free - L'oiseau Bleu
Criminal Officium, Geoid Color Circle, Cocktail synesthésique, Techno Thriller, Legion 808, Air Likör

19 March 2018
RUMSTEEK
Santé Loisirs présente:
Zach Phillips, Loto Retina, frere tuck

23 March 2018
ATELIERS CLAUS
Nina Harker, W Ravenveer / dj Marouchka Payen, expo Erwin Van Looveren

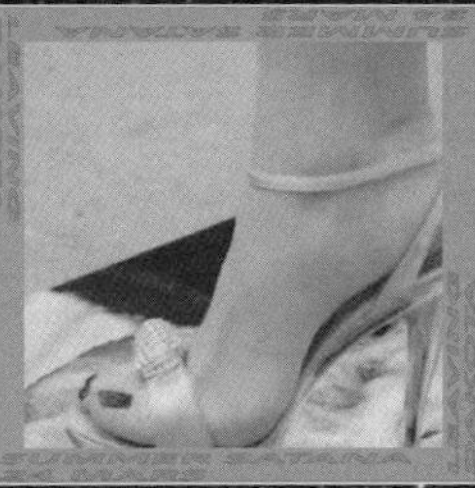

24 March 2018
LES BRASSERIES ATLAS
Xanax & Mazarance IV, Kurama, Pavel, Summer Satana

A puzzle of hearsay about bars, cafés and regular parties for lesbians in Brussels, in approximate chronology. The hearsay and hearts are gathered during the ongoing research of Brussels Almanack Lesbian (BAL).

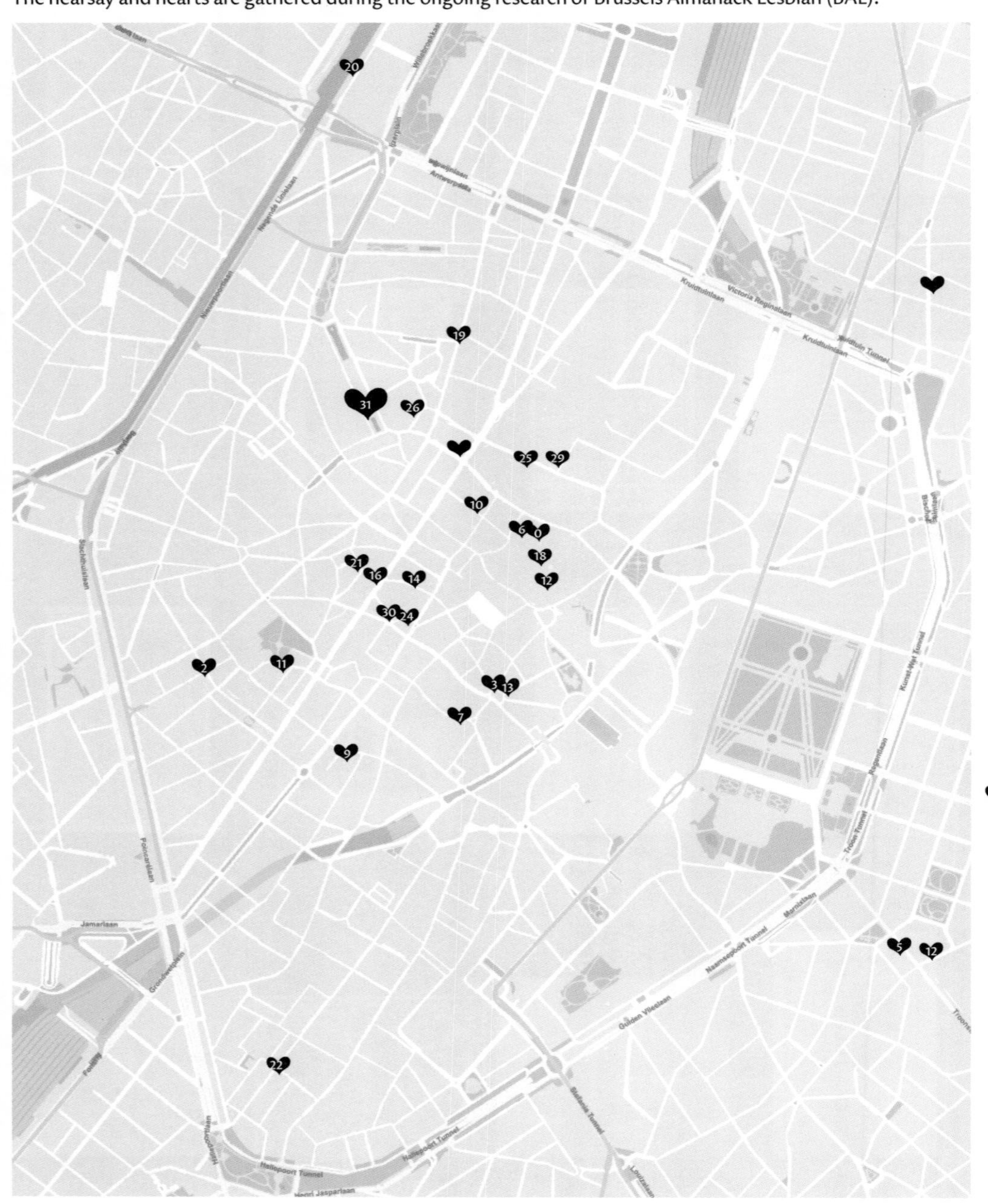

Hetero guys could pay extra to be allowed to stare at or touch lesbians. Sometimes we actually danced them out! Pushed them back out onto the street by just taking back the dancefloor. There was a feeling of freedom to kick them out!

All black everything. People did not want to be recognized. No funny lights, very sombre. I couldn't exist in it, it was terrible that way. It did not feel like home. It was located in a remote street, and you had to know when it was open. That was risky. But some people were just happy it existed at all.

It was about taking up public space. There was a piano, there were events, lectures. The bar had a big mirror behind it, and above that hung a very large portrait of Virginia Wolf.

We called the owner 'Mae West'.

Very dark.

Where the lesbian magazine *De Paarse Peperpot* first started.

Too hardcore.

It had a mix of men and women. And a lot of 'prostitutes'. Non-professional prostitutes.

Sociologically it was great. All the female bus- and tram-conductors at the time were lesbians, and they had these very femme girlfriends that would come to the bar just after midnight to wait for their butch partners to finish work. Also it was the first time I saw someone in a wheelchair in a bar. Yes the bar was dodgy, but it was also inclusive and open.

late 1950s	1 **la Pergola**
late 1960s	2 **Unnamed café in Loofstraat**
1980–82?	3 **Elle (later Amfora)**
ca 1978	4 **Lilith**
ca 1978	5 **Liever Eva**
parties ca 1979	**Homo-L**
early 1980s	6 **Black Swan**
early 1980s	7 **Le Chewing-gum bar** ?
early 1980s	8 **Le Cercle** ?
around 1985	9 **Lady June** (cafe)
Wednesdays 1987	10 **De Kluts**
1990?–94	11 **Le Capricorne**
12 11 1981–83	12 **Madam / Le Madam Club**
01 08 1982–?	13 **Amfora (old Elle)**
–	14 **L'Evenement**
–	**La Lune**
1990-97?	16 **Le Féminin**
1990	17 **Sappholie**
around 1990	18 **Diamant Rose**
around 1990	19 **Club Radical** ?
monthly 1995–98	20 **La Peniche**
around 1998	21 **Sapho**
1995-1999	22 **D-LIGHT / Pussy Galore**
Parties ca 1999	**Les Biches**
-	24 **The Big Noise**
Saturdays 1998–99	25 **Womania**
ca 2000	26 **Wings**
ca 2000	27 **Le Bistrot Lesbien**
2000-2003	28 **Lespace**
1999-2003	29 **Gate**
2001-ongoing	30 **Rainbow House**
May-June 2018	31 **Mothers & Daughters**

Very dark, but more open as a space.

Chic!

Fancy, more expensive. To enter you had to know the number and which doorbell to ring, which was secret. However, you also had to write your full name and address in a register! I told all the young lesbians to write fake names. The place was not politically critical, but commercial, and so it felt wrong that they had a list of our names.

Ran by Jackie, a very good chef. Delicious. It was a café & restaurant until 22:00 and then it became a bar. Jackie recognized the struggle of being a lesbian. She was from a well-off family, but had not had it easy. She was very protective of the lesbian, chosen family, but also she and her partner must have been one of the first lesbian couples to have a baby.

Mostly heavy cruising was my impression.

The last place for a long while that was not mainly commercial but took care of the community. There were a lot of lesbian regulars.

A man with a moustache would stand guard at the door. You had to pay him as you went out, for protection. He was often together with a blonde woman who would always make sure you had a drink.

At the back a dark room that wasn't a dark room...

A café ran by Bizoux, a well-known DJ among all the Brussels lesbians.

The Bistro, it was almost a discussion group. A place for philosophy and reflection.

A reaction against the small bars. Large lesbian parties were organized, forming a club that used the membership cards to avoid the police. The law protected us, but the police didn't. The gays would follow the trend. It was always like that. We were runaways and outcasts, always creating new types of social spaces.

It was inclusive. I would be there at 5 in the morning and a group of Moroccan girls would come dancing for example. We didn't have many places like that.

Good music. A self-determined resistance inside the LGBT scene. Saw itself as a moving star. Mixed. Very queer.

They invited bands, it was a lot of fun.

One of the most important (impressive) parties I ever saw. At the time we must have had the biggest lesbian parties in Europe. There were 800 lesbians.

Oh the boat! 'no-man's-land'

I wouldn't say 800, I would say 400. But they were big.

Ah, yes, Carieneke's place.

Zuidstraat * Lombardstraat

Kolenmarkt

Flageyplein

Schumanplein

After I had fled Gaza and finally arrived in Brussels, I fell in love with the freedom of the city. I noticed numerous couples of various backgrounds walking together, holding hands and embracing each other in public. To me this shows freedom.

PARIS XL

Khalil Masood

OTHER FREEDOMS THAT I WASN'T USED TO

Cinema in public

Women on a bike

Drinking alcohol

Circus in public

Dancing in public

Concerts in public

Women behind the tap

Statues in the city

International books

Parks in the city

Sorted waste

Kissing in public

Walking the dog

Trains as public transport

Mixed gym

International brands

Lisemarie Van Loon

ROUTES TO BRUSSELS

Through the experiences with my Bolivian boyfriend and the stories of international friends, I was confronted with many facets regarding immigration and integration in Belgium on a daily level. I interviewed five persons who fled their country and made this map with the information they were willing to share — for which I'm very grateful. Khalil, Yusuf, Haytham, Jafeer and Kamal allowed me to look through their eyes on our Western way of living and how they deal with that. These encounters taught me a lot in many aspects and I've experienced how other worlds are very nearby.

Haytham (25)

from Gaza, Palestine to Brussels 07 2016 → 09 2016

Haytham came to Brussels to reunite with his father and brother in the first place. Nowadays, he lives on his own and learned Dutch in a short time. He's looking for opportunities to fulfil his training in Electrical engineering.

Jafeer (34)

from Baghdad, Iraq via Brussels to Antwerp 04 2014 → 11 2014

Jafeer came 'accidentally' to Belgium because of his fake passport with Belgian nationality. Once he arrived in Brussels, he got help in the asylum centre and is now living in Antwerp and working as an artist.

Kamal (32)

from Lattakia, Syria to Brussels 11 2015 → 09 2016

Kamal heard many stories from his older brother who started a new family and life in Belgium. When the war forced him to flee Syria, his only destination in mind was Brussels. He used to work in a laboratory, but he can't find work because his diploma is not valid here. Instead he's improving his French and learning Dutch.

Khalil (28)

from Gaza, Palestine to Brussels 09 2016 → 01 2017

Khalil came to Brussels because he heard from his friends, who lived there, a lot of good things about this city. He loves the freedom and social events that Brussels has to offer. Khalil currently works as a freelance photographer.

Yusuf (28)

from Lasgar Gah, Afghanistan, via Brussels to Antwerp 07 2013 → 04 2014

Yusuf had a dream to go and live in Sweden but arrived in Brussels instead. He discovered many opportunities for his future, and finally decided to live close to his friend in Antwerp, after having worked for a long time as an interpreter in Brussels.

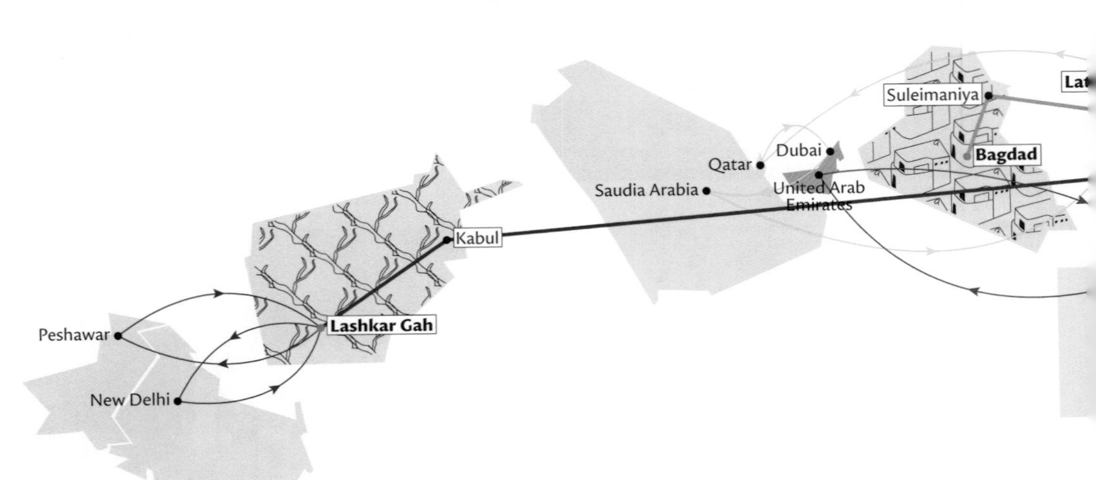

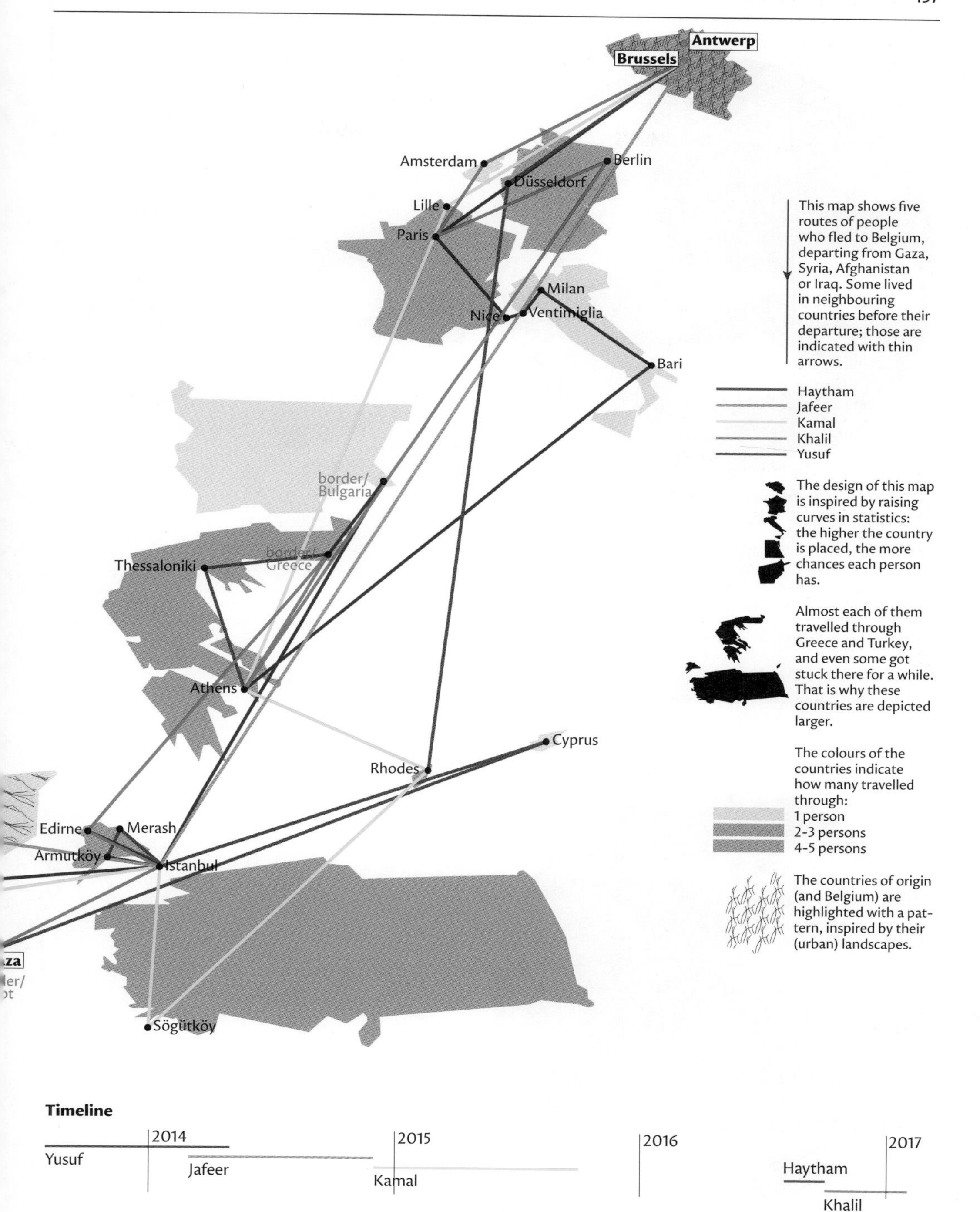
Antwerp
Brussels
Amsterdam
Berlin
Düsseldorf
Lille
Paris
Milan
Nice
Ventimiglia
Bari
border/
Bulgaria
border/
Greece
Thessaloniki
Athens
Cyprus
Rhodes
Edirne
Merash
Armutköy
Istanbul
Sögütköy
This map shows five routes of people who fled to Belgium, departing from Gaza, Syria, Afghanistan or Iraq. Some lived in neighbouring countries before their departure; those are indicated with thin arrows.
Haytham
Jafeer
Kamal
Khalil
Yusuf
The design of this map is inspired by raising curves in statistics: the higher the country is placed, the more chances each person has.
Almost each of them travelled through Greece and Turkey, and even some got stuck there for a while. That is why these countries are depicted larger.
The colours of the countries indicate how many travelled through:
1 person
2-3 persons
4-5 persons
The countries of origin (and Belgium) are highlighted with a pattern, inspired by their (urban) landscapes.

Timeline

2014
2015
2016
2017
Yusuf
Jafeer
Kamal
Haytham
Khalil

Saraa Saleh, *Academic, artist*
1000, Brussels
Brussels, like Damascus, cannot be neutral and my relationship with them cannot be serene. To really live in such a city means to be engaged with it in a passionate and yet complex relationship.

Yasser Al-Sarraj, *Owner of Bab Al-Hara restaurant*
1070, Anderlecht
Dear Brussels, I came to you from the eastern coast of the Mediterranean, to you I present the most delightful inventions of this coast.

Mahmoud Saber, *Nuts shopkeeper*
1070, Anderlecht
In Syria, roasting, flavouring and mixing nuts is considered an art, not a profession.

Emad Karkokly, *Sweets shopkeeper*
1000, Brussels
The sweetest of Damascus in the heart of Brussels.

Kito Sino, *Artist*
1030, Schaerbeek
Everywhere I went, I carried Brussels with me
and left a part of it behind.

Angela Al-Souliman, *Video artist*
1210, Saint-Josse
Brussels, I will blossom in you as
the jasmine blossoms in a Syrian spring.

Katia Al Jbrail,
Sr Specialist Regulatory Oversight Management
1060, Saint-Gilles
Brussels, my love, I know your lanes
as I know the lines in the palm of my hand.

Nirit Peled

KINDRED SPIRITS

As an immigrant from the Middle East I always feel uprooted. 20 years in Amsterdam gave me a hard time finding communities that are inclusive to my identity. But in the safe space of *Le Space* I found an inclusive family of misfits which gave me the belonging I was looking for. Monthly I make my way to the city that gave birth to this radical independent scene, which is blessed with characters that keep reminding me of the colourful world we live in. I learned that we all took long roads to get there and that we are happy to claim the cities we reside in while declining the state and the national identity that come with it. This map is a tribute to some of those that I met in *Le Space* and the worlds they come from. This is a group I have been encountering in Brussels, people I know and recognize. I finally find rest in the ideas that my people, with their colours and language different than mine, can be kindred spirits. I realize that right there between these people I can be at peace with this, my chosen European exile.

Gia Abrassart
Lodja · Dour · Brussels · Luanda · Nairobi · Genève · Salvador De Bahia · Brussels
Gia is a decolonizing-cultural activist and journalist. With Lise she forms the collective Warrior Poets. Together they connect the dots and combine life and love in a way that is contagious. As an Afro-entrepreneur, Gia has just launched her label Ginger G, a fresh homemade ginger elixir infused with lemon, spices & love. Best to drink when Lise is spinning feminine voices of our generation.

Harmony Benegusenga
Kigali · Neirobi · Kessel-Lo · Leuven · Brussels
I am African; no doubt, Harmony declares. African born, African raised, she even carries the Messiah clarification which is burned on her skin. Yet she also calls herself a *Leuvenaar*. There everything started. The birth of her creative self. Combining her passion for cameras and the great imagination she has had in her since childhood. A film-maker was born.

Santo Domingo

Christophe Callewaert
Ruiselede · Tielt · Ghent · Kinshasa · Leuven · Brussels
Christophe is co-founder and journalist at *De Wereld Morgen*, Rachida's husband and father of 10-year-old Miel. A critical thinker, in his book 'Dit is Morgen' he relates all his pessimistic observations in the intro. Yet he spends the rest of his words on inspiring ideas of change that can make a better future for his family.

Elisabeth Severino Fernandes
Bragança · Santo Domingo · Madrid · Ghent · Antwerp · Brussels
Also known as 'Godmother of Poetry' she is an activist, curator and a spoken word artist. Too dark to be *protégées*, too light Dominican, too Portuguese to be Spanish and too Belgian to be anything else. She feels like an immigrant everywhere. From this intersection she works to create spaces where women and people of colour get a prominent place.

Naïma Isabelle Moldenhauer
Bougaa · Sétif · Limburg · Antwerp
Is a visual (he-)artist, traveller, lover of nature. Born and raised in Antwerp. A daughter to a Belgian father and Algerian mother she was raised as Isabelle Moldenhauer. Only when enrolling in university did she use her first name Naïma which made her rethink her gaze.

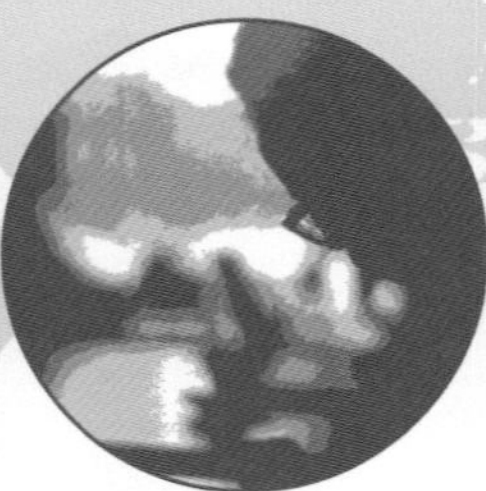

Lyse Okoye Ishimwe
Kigali · Windhoek · Brussels · Tubize
Lyse is a photographer, curator and film enthusiast. With vivid excitement she relates the latest films and shares contagious dreams of founding a film festival in Ruanda. Currently she is the founder and curator of Recognition, a programme that aims to increase the visibility of African and African diaspora art, literature and culture via community-based film screenings, workshops

Lise Vanderpiete
Wingene · Torhout · Ghent · Brussels
Lise is a librarian and community builder. As co-founder of the Brussels-based collective Warrior Poets, she and Gia were my introduction to everyone I've met in the city. They invited me at first time to Brussels to screen a film about women and hip-hop. A gifted organizer of youth and urban arts, Lise is best to meet on the dance floor as a devoted music selector.

Salvador De Bahia

Rachida Aziz

Berkane · Antwerp · Brussels

Rachida is an opinionated fashion designer, writer and the founder of the hybrid art and culture café *Le Space*. The ground level store used to be a fashion boutique, located in the commercial district in Brussels but is now designed to contain radical thinkers and misfits of society. Rachida's plea for radicalization is bundled with love and inclusivity.

Nirit Peled

Sanaa · Haleb · Rehovot · Tel aviv · Amsterdam

Nomadic storyteller in constant search of new ideas and old stories. Navigating between different worlds and identities and to find a place for a half-Yemeni, half-Syrian, Israeli artist who used to believe in God, but now believes in dreams.

Sunny afternoon, 25 June 2018

BANNERS FOR REALLY
DULL EXPOS THAT NOBODY VISITS
LOVES TO EAT
Bald
Long hair
Big Belly
CRAZY GUY PULLING HIS T-SHIRT BEHIND HIS HEAD, SHOWING HIS BELLY
HAS TO LISTEN
IS ALWAYS HERE & ALWAYS SAYS NO
RASTAMAN ROLLING A JOINT
LOUD
GUYS WEARING WINTER COATS IN 27°C
MUSLIM WOMAN SMOKING WITH A MAN
YOUNG TEEN-AGE BOY = SO CHILL
Family? FRIENDS?
GOOD KID MAKING FUNNY FACES & CHECKING WHO'S WATCHING THEM
ADMIRING
MAGAZINE-PRETTY GIRL WITH STRAIGHTENED HAIR & F.Me BOOTS
TODDLER DISCOVERING PIGEON CHASING
OLD SPANISH LADY WITH POODLE SHOES.

Casual Chic
Abdel Doudou Medoki *(Fashion Blogger)*

Classic
Roland Abgobli

Classic with a proud message

Trendsetter
(Singer)

Dandy
Danny Ngobo *(Athlete)*

Dandy
Jean Michel Eklu *(Researcher)*

Dandy
Clyde Baron *(Stylish)*

Eclectic Sophisticated
Gessica *(Psychologist)* & Siré Kaba *(Designer)*

Classic
DJ Steeve & Benito *(Style coach)*

Casual Chic
Friend & Ousman Fofanah *(Designer)*

Ankara

Business
Alphonse Muambi (*Writer*)

Off - White Outfit
Trendsetter

Dandy
Etienne Kabongo (*Activist*)

Dandy

Trendsetter
Cries Sauvage (*Artist*)

Tribal Bold

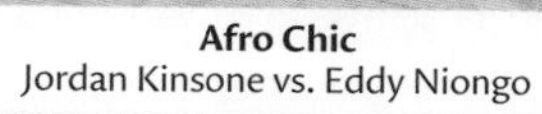

Afro Chic
Jordan Kinsone vs. Eddy Niongo

Casual Chic
Jovita *(Singer)*

Eclectic Statement
Siré Kaba *(Designer)* & Abdel Doudou Medoki

Schuman metro
(European Quarter)
Monday 15 May 2017
08:32–09:08am

F	𝍸 𝍸 |||	B	𝍸 |||	I	𝍸
D	𝍸 𝍸	GB	𝍸 |	NL	𝍸
ES	𝍸 ||||	PL	𝍸 |	CZ	||||

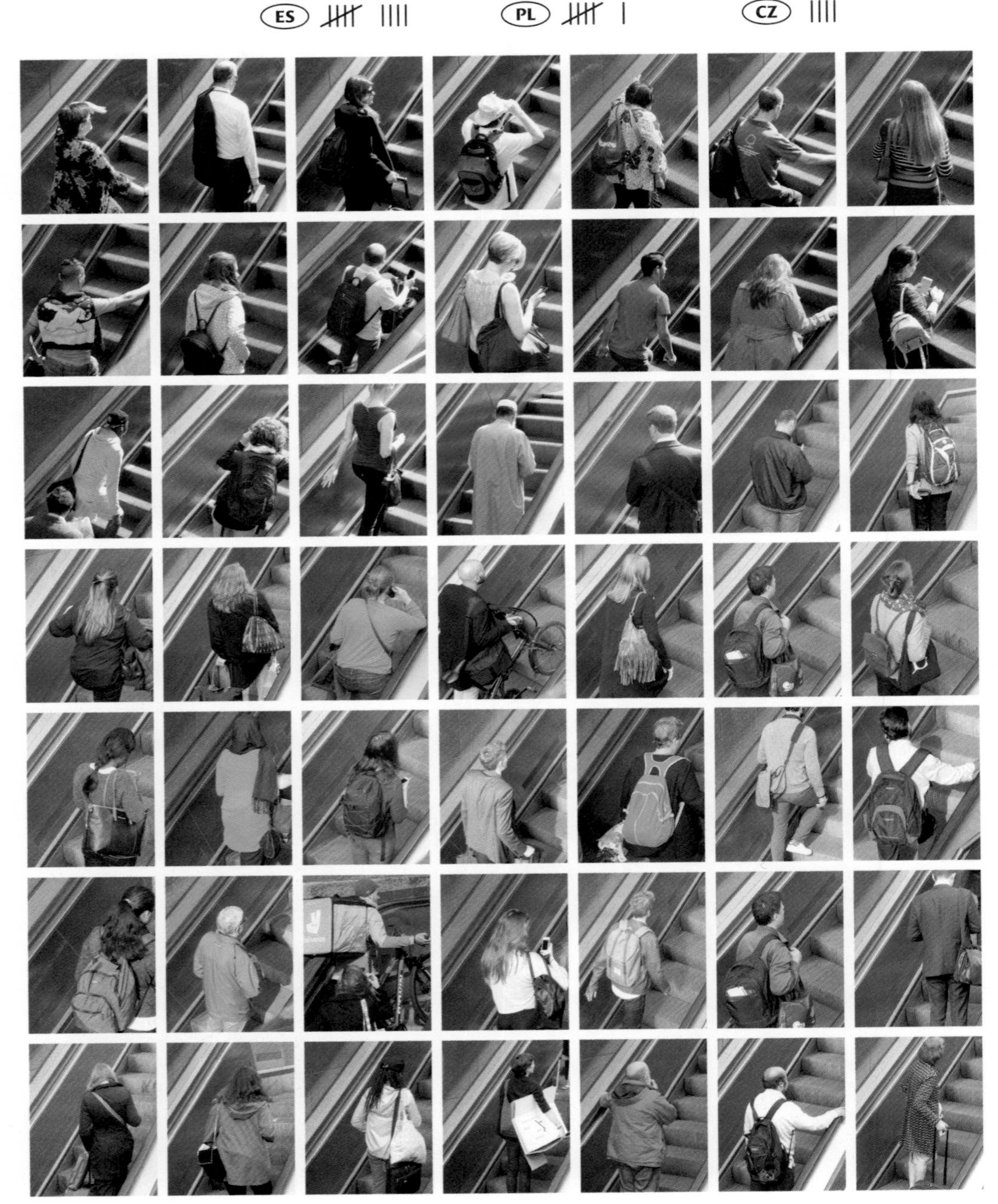

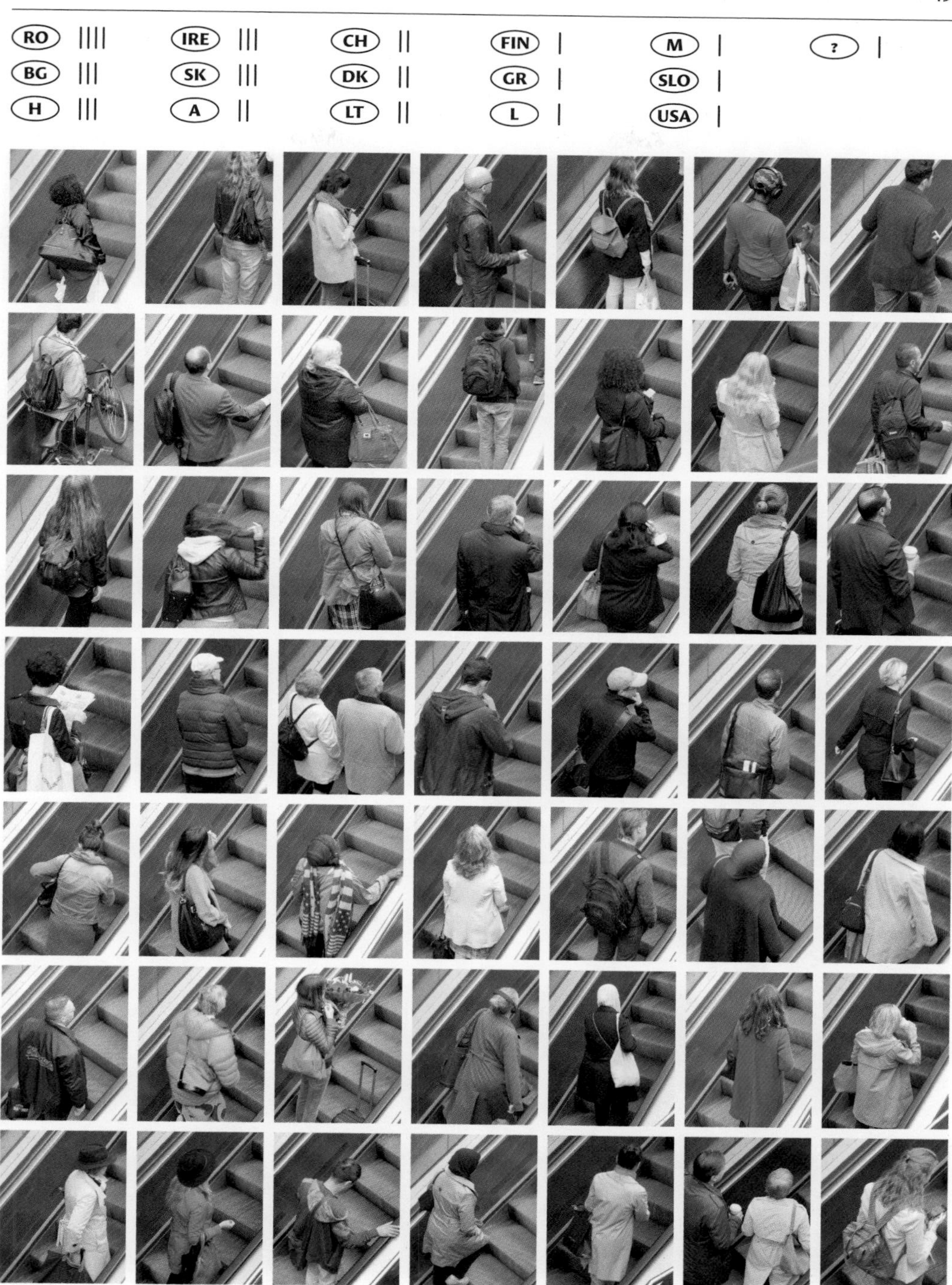
RO ||||
BG |||
H |||
IRE |||
SK |||
A ||
CH ||
DK ||
LT ||
FIN |
GR |
L |
M |
SLO |
USA |
? |

DIVERGENT

Karel Goethals

OUT OF THE LUNCHBOX

Brussels is Belgium's top destination for commuters – I was one myself before I moved to the city centre. Each day, about 350,000 people travel to the Belgian capital for work and with them, they often bring their homemade lunchbox. Especially among the Flemish city workers, their so-called *brooddoos* is a classic on their

Dominique (61) *Management assistant*
6 km by bus and metro

Carla (58) *Event hostess*
7 km by car or bus

Guido (60) *Camera man and artist*
8 km by bike

Anton (43) *Counselor for job seekers*
11 km by bike

Anneke (42) *HR legal counsel*
12 km by bike

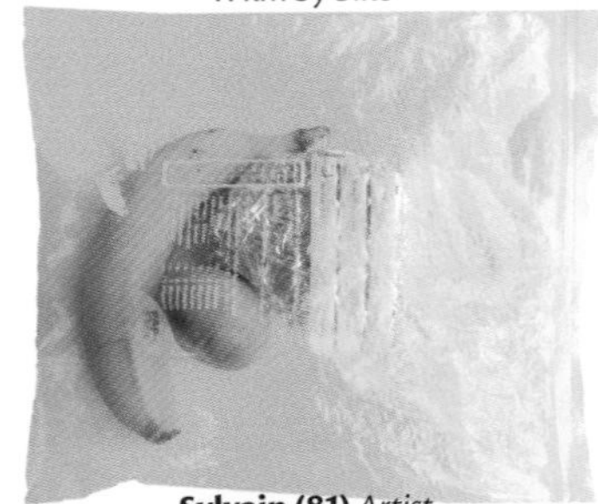

Sylvain (81) *Artist*
12 km by car

Florence (30) *Legal counsel*
14 km by car or train

Levin (37) *Banker*
15 km by train

weekly menu. It is a culinary tradition that has always fascinated me, so I asked sixteen commuters from all ages to unbox their lunch for me.

Sofie (35) *Insurance broker*
16 km by car

Kris (49) *Student advisor*
19 km by car or bike

Pascale (55) *HR Consultant*
23 km by car

Klaas (25) *Lawyer*
30 km by car

Melanie (33) *Policy advisor residential care*
34 km by train and folding bike

Wilfried (40) *Art teacher and artist*
60 km by train or car

Georges (71) *Artist at art academy*
60 km by car

Luco (30) *Conversation manager*
105 km by car

GREEK
with oregano and bay leaf

CYPRIOTIC
with lentils, hiromeri (smoked ham) and Commandaria wine

MEDITERRANEAN
with balsamic glaze and parmesan

ITALIAN
with truffles and Pecorino

SPANISH
with spicy chorizo and spices

ITALIAN
with pancetta and thyme

MIDDLE EASTERN
with mandarine, celery and almond nuts

FINISHED PLATE

WHITE WINE
HALF EN HALF
half and half
SPARKLING WINE
DUVEL
DUIKBOOT
submarine
DUTCH GIN
ORANGE JUICE
MACHINE TRUC
TONIC
GRAPEFRUIT JUICE
ESKIMO | CHOSE
TONIC
BEER
MAZOET
fuel oil
COKE
BEER
TANGO
GRENADINE
WHITE WINE
HOER
whore
HOEGAARDEN
KRIEK
VUILE HOER
dirty whore
HOEGAARDEN

BAGUETTE

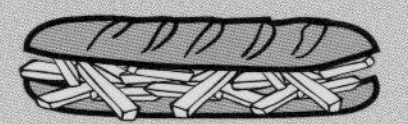
MITRAILLETTE
machine gun

FRIES

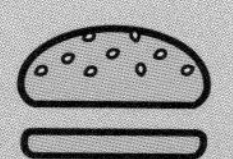
BIKY BUN

BICKY KEFTA
bicky (hamburger) kefta

KEFTA BURGER

TOMATO

TOMAT CREVETTE
tomato shrimp

LITTLE SHRIMPS

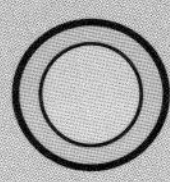
PEACH

PECHE TONIJN
peach tuna

TUNA

PRUNES

KONIJN PRUIMEN
rabbit with prunes

RABBIT

CHICORY

HESP WITLOOF
ham chicory

HAM

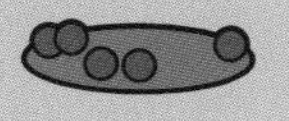
CHERRIES

BALLEKES KRIEKSKES
meatbal cherries

MEATBALL

BEEF STEW

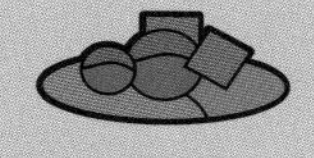
TROG
feed-box for pigs

MEATBAL WITH TOMATO

Is the canal a mental border? Does it separate two different cultural identities? I started out by visiting the first shop and café next to the bridge. As I got the chance to meet shopowners I asked them to connect me with another entrepreneur on the street who they work with.

MOLENBEEK

Belbo, *Mohammed Nadim*

Noisette boulangerie, *Souleyman*

Shop Sahin, *Sahin*

Nazar, *Haji*

Ideal Cash & Carry, *Mohammed Asaf*

Shark Coiffure, *Said Ali*

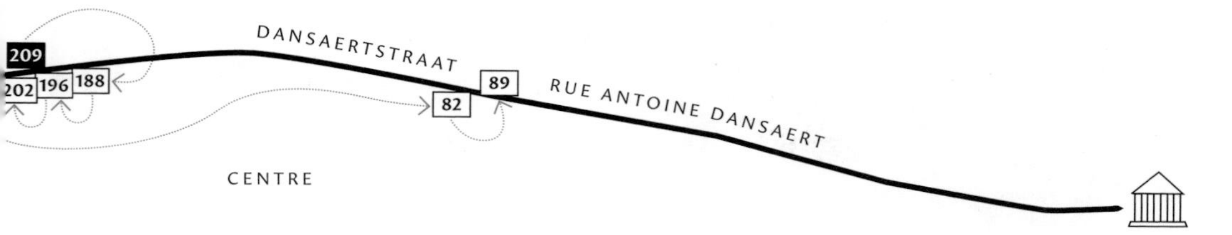

De Walvis, *Astrid*

Brussels Beer Project, *Stefano*

MOK, coffee roastery, *Jens*

La Belle Equipe, *Matthias & Eva*

L'imperial Grillades, *Laila*

Kim Boutique, *Sana & Soumaya & Miriam,*

open 6pm–2am, closed on thursdays
origin: Pakistan

open 6pm–2am, closed on tuesdays
origin: Pakistan

open all days 6pm–3am
origin: Bangladesh

open all days 6pm–4am
origin: Nepal

open 6pm–6am, sundays closed
origin: Nepal

open 6pm–2am, sundays closed
origin: Pakistan

Céline Callens

open all days 6pm – 2am
origin: India

Céline Callens

open all days 6pm – 2am
origin: India

Pieterjan Volckaert

open all days 6pm – 3am
origin: Pakistan

Jorge de la Torre

open all days 10am–12pm
origin: Pakistan

Erika Sprey

open all days 6pm–1am
origin: Pakistan

Erika Sprey

open all days 4pm–2am
origin: India

When I moved from Jerusalem to Brussels, I was living in Yser. The closest swimming pool was in the Marolles, that's how I came to know the Marché aux Puces at Place du Jeu de Balle. I fell in love with the neighbourhood and the energy that this place contained; people crying out loud, negotiating prices. It reminded me of Palestine, a lot.

When searching in the cartons, one can find old family photos, paintings and notebooks – old memories, being sold on the streets, for passers-by to rummage through. I moved houses twice, and the first thing I look for when moving is the distance between my new house and the Place du Jeu de Balle. I feel that I belong in that street, with all these memories.

Flea markets and antique shops are still full of tangible items from the colonial past. Waiting for a second life, these objects are for a short period visible to everyone, like an open window onto the past. From luxurious sculpted ivory items which have lost their value to decorative statues representing slaves, these goods carry with them part of the darkest history of Belgium.

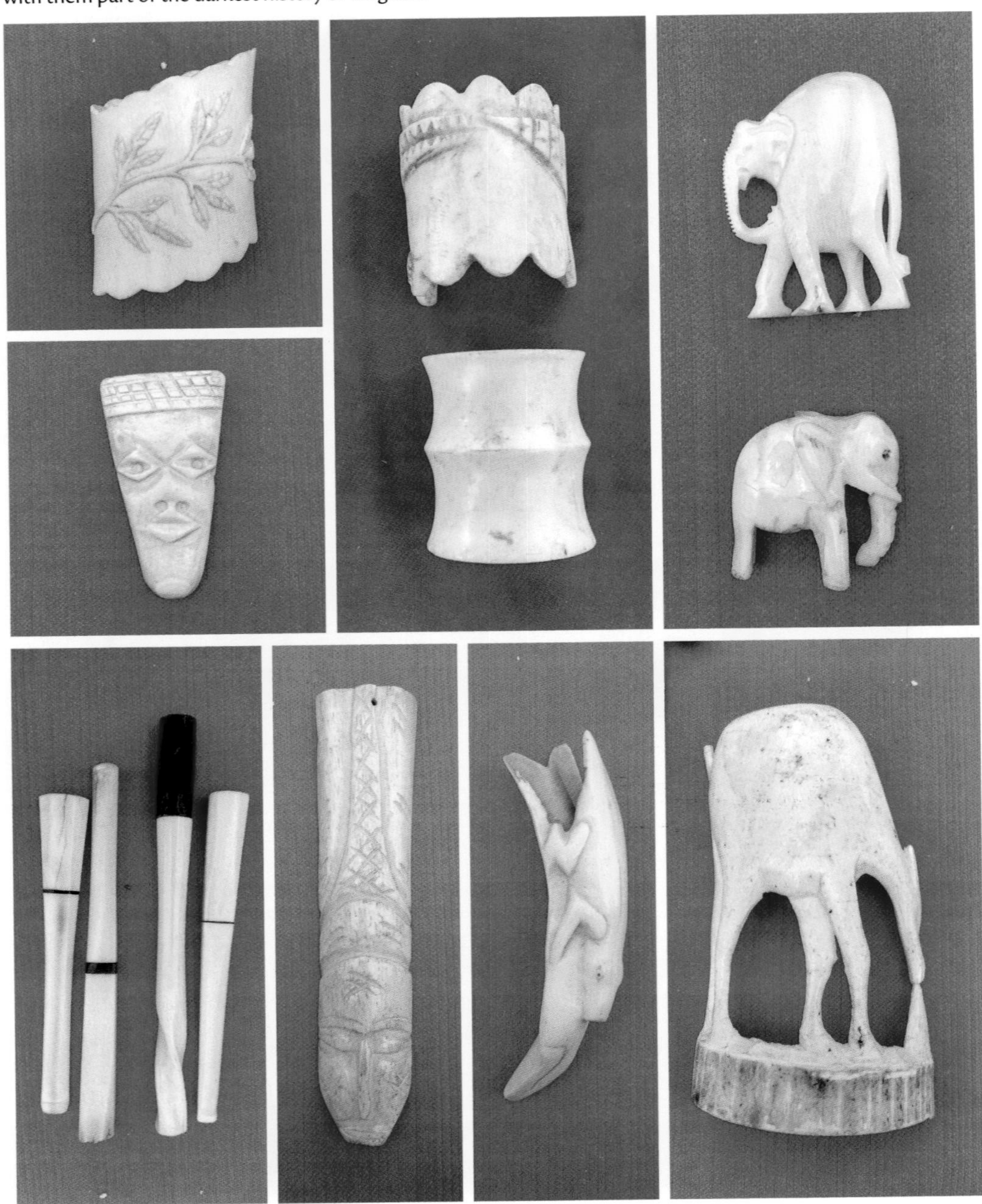

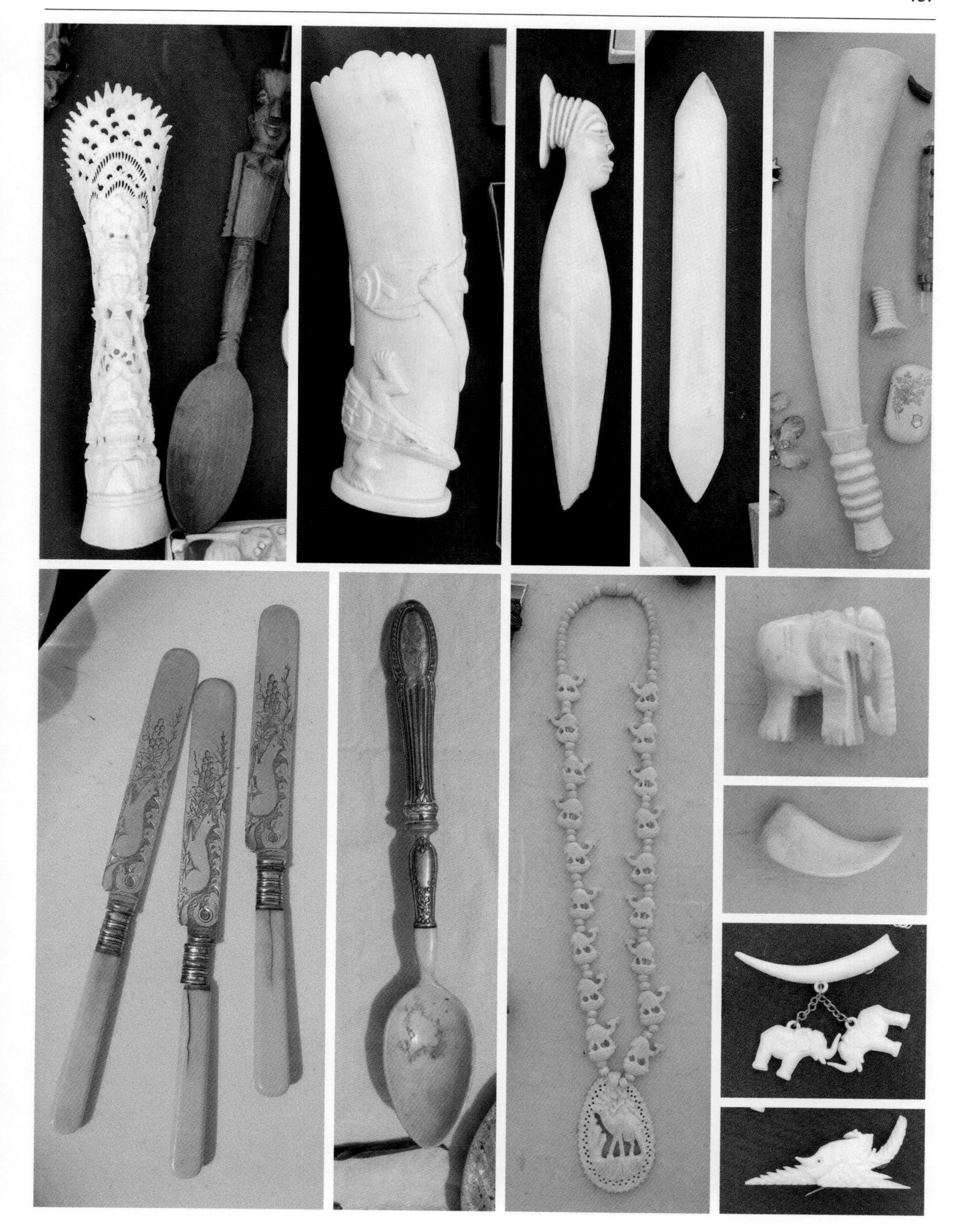

Granito, 1190 Vorst

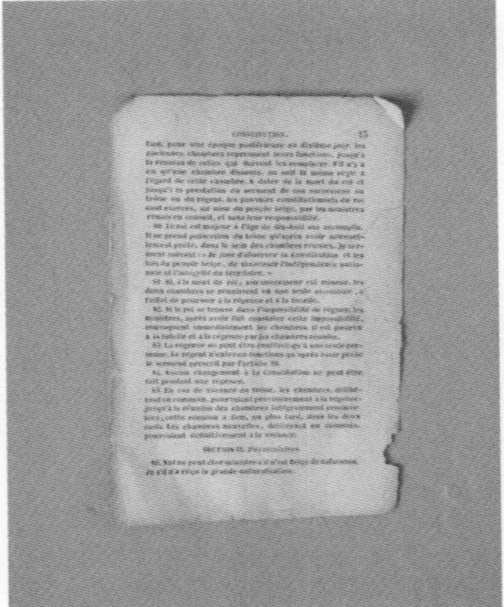

Constitution, 1000 Brussels

Orient, 1000 Brussels

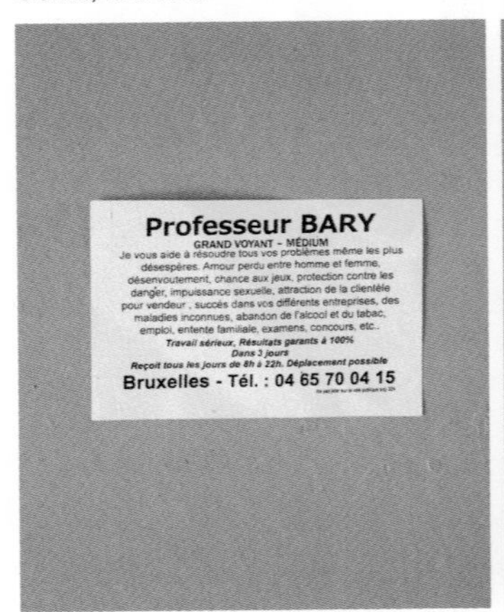

Professeur BARY, 1190 Vorst

Pigeon Life, Park van Vorst

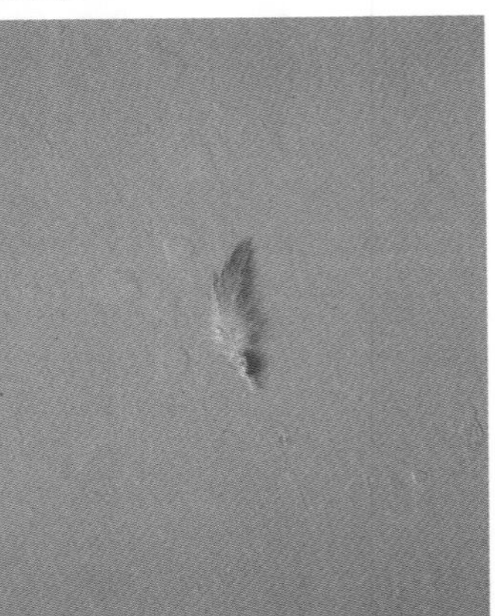

Since 1974, Park van Vorst

Bien Mangé, 1000 Brussels

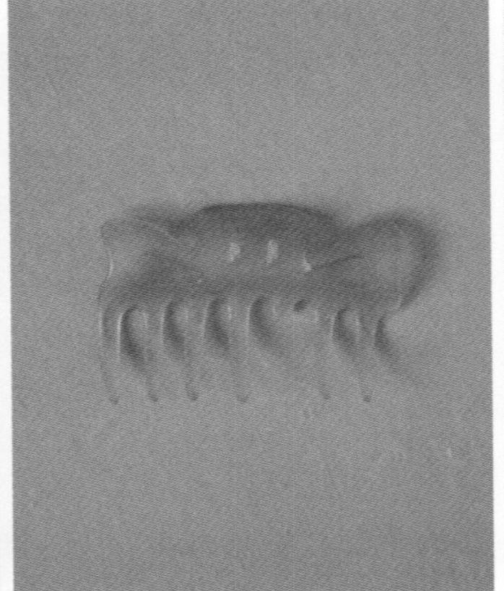

Dysfunctional, 1000 Brussels

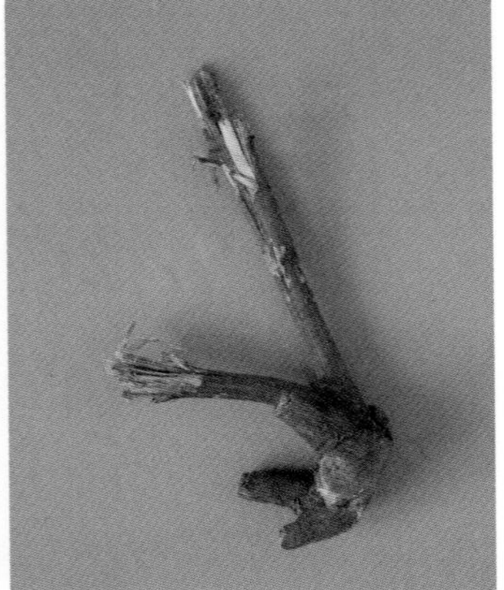

Beech, Dudenpark

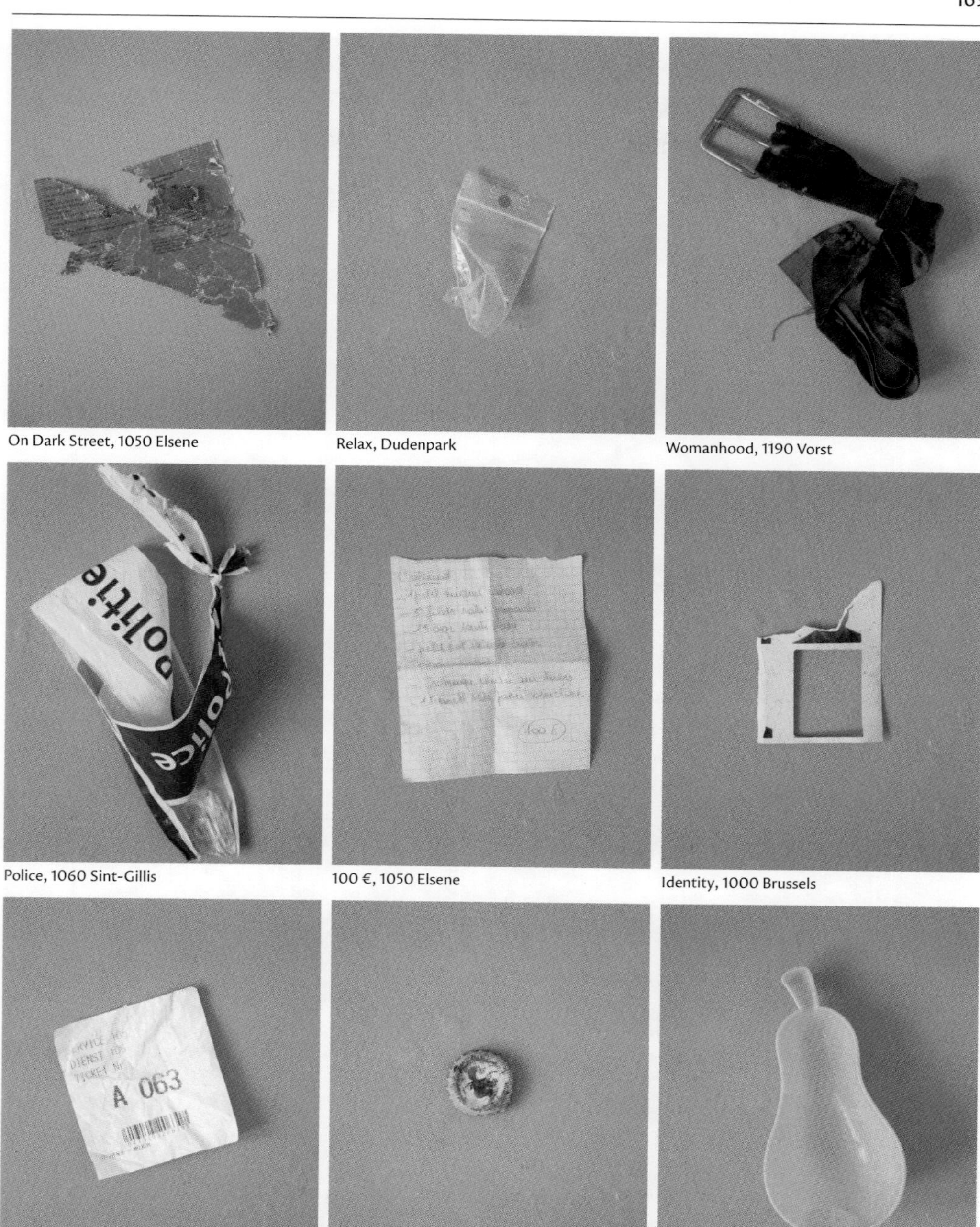

On Dark Street, 1050 Elsene

Relax, Dudenpark

Womanhood, 1190 Vorst

Police, 1060 Sint-Gillis

100 €, 1050 Elsene

Identity, 1000 Brussels

Service - Dienst -Ticket, 1190 Vorst

La Chouffe, Park van Vorst

Ketje, Park van Vorst

After the attacks on 22 March 2016, the *Beursplein* transformed into a national commemoration place of mourning, solidarity and unity. It was a powerful signal, not chosen from above but by citizens who started to

write on the ground, burned candles and gathered collectively. It was a grand act of activism, to reclaim the public street and mark the square as a commemoration of unity in variety and a place for political expression.

Christiane Högner

NEW GENERATION OF BRUSSELEIRS

One of the outstanding characteristics of Brussels in general is the multitude of different cultural backgrounds that live side by side. This is an enourmous wealth on the one side – especially for the next generations who grow up in the middle of different mother tongues and of various local interpretations of shared rituals. Yet it can also be a source of mis-communication and of a growing detachment, since almost everyone is also oriented to a family or a context beyond Brussels and Belgium. The classmates of our seven year old daughter, all attending a regular public school, illustrate that perfectly when mapping their individual family backgrounds.

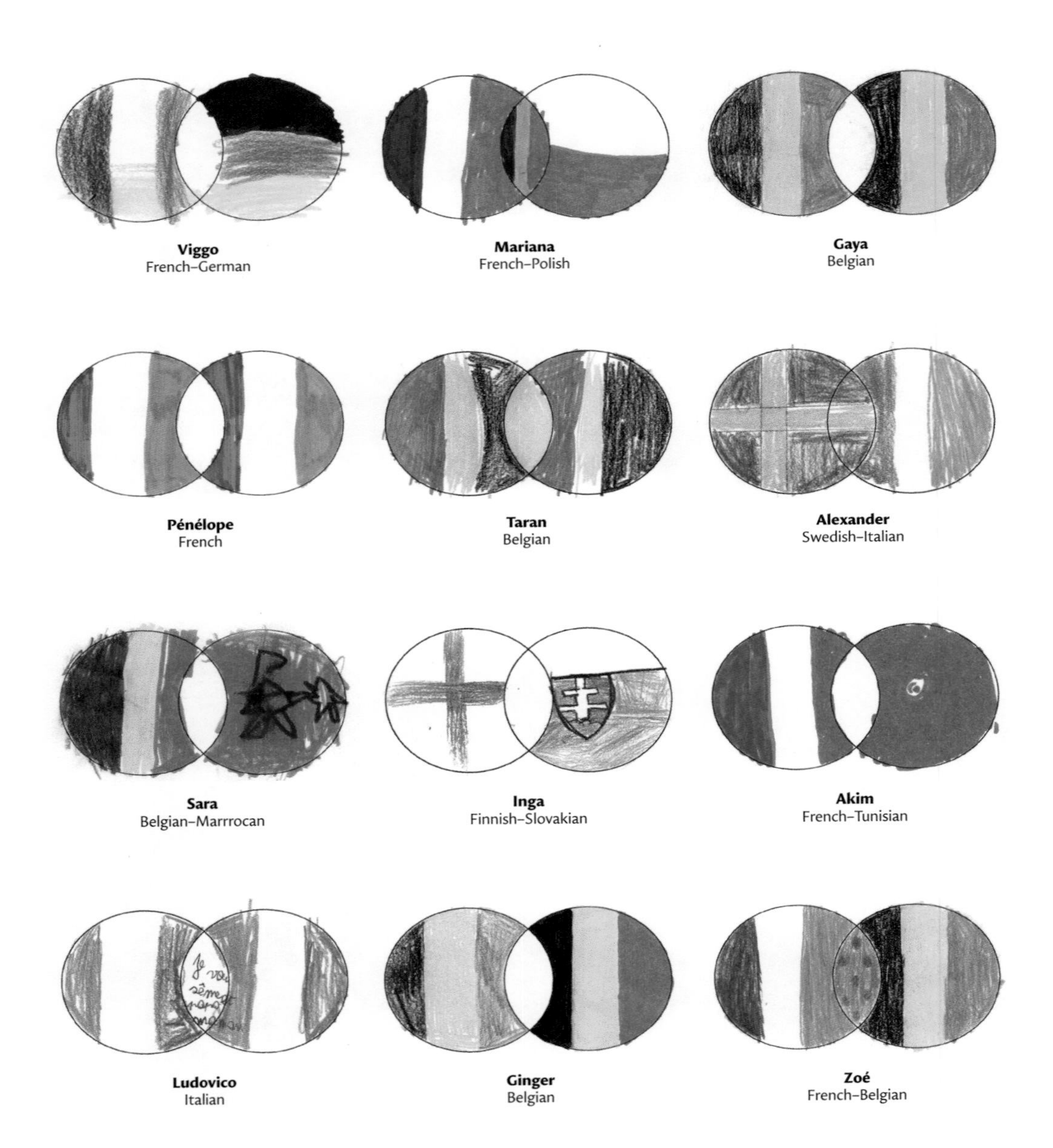

Viggo
French–German

Mariana
French–Polish

Gaya
Belgian

Pénélope
French

Taran
Belgian

Alexander
Swedish–Italian

Sara
Belgian–Marrrocan

Inga
Finnish–Slovakian

Akim
French–Tunisian

Ludovico
Italian

Ginger
Belgian

Zoé
French–Belgian

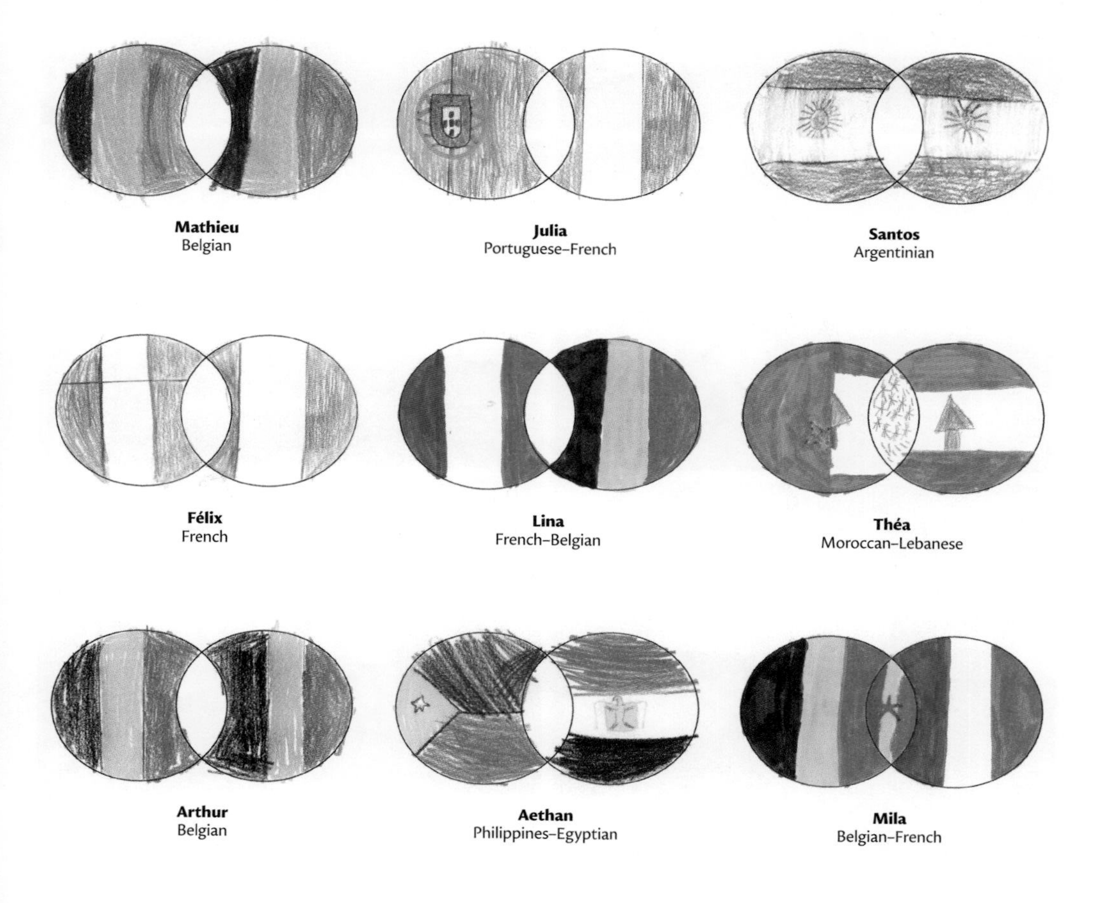

Mathieu
Belgian

Julia
Portuguese–French

Santos
Argentinian

Félix
French

Lina
French–Belgian

Théa
Moroccan–Lebanese

Arthur
Belgian

Aethan
Philippines–Egyptian

Mila
Belgian–French

Emilia
German–Belgian

VIVA LALGERI
BELGIUM
MUTUALITE SOCIALISTE
SOCIALISTISCHE MUTUALITEIT

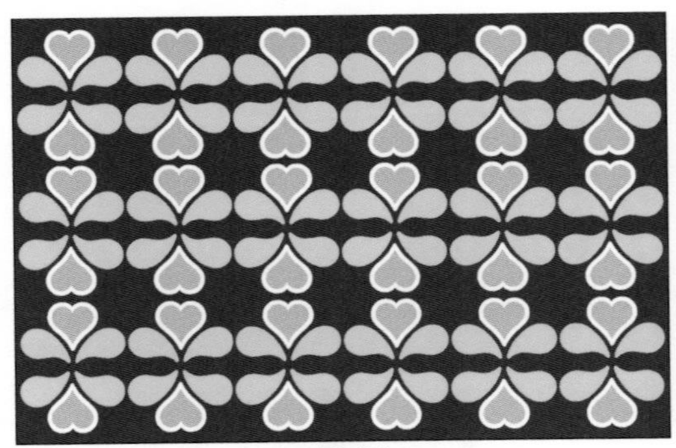

Multiplicity
Joud Toamah

L'iris de Bruxelles
Amina Saâdi

Brussels Air, evolutive flag
Jorge de la Torre

Brussels Unlimited
Caroline Dath *(Kidnap your designer)*

Superimposition
Omar Kashmiry

Hope
Sophie Feyder

Under Construction
Riitta Oittinen

Liberty
Anonymous

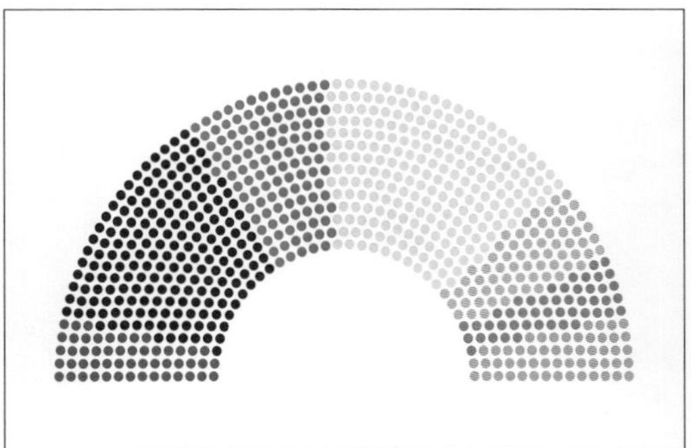

Equal parliament
Vos Broekema

Proud
Celine Callens

Multiculti
Lucie Pinier

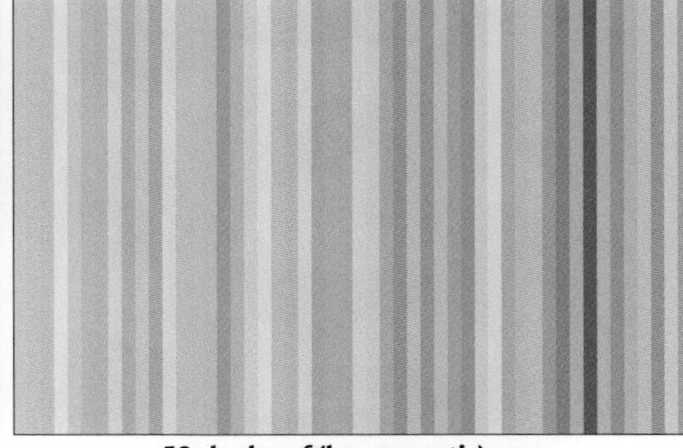

50 shades of (bureaucratic) grey
Hendrik Jan Grievink

One
Germaine Kruip

Triumph
Omar Kashmiry

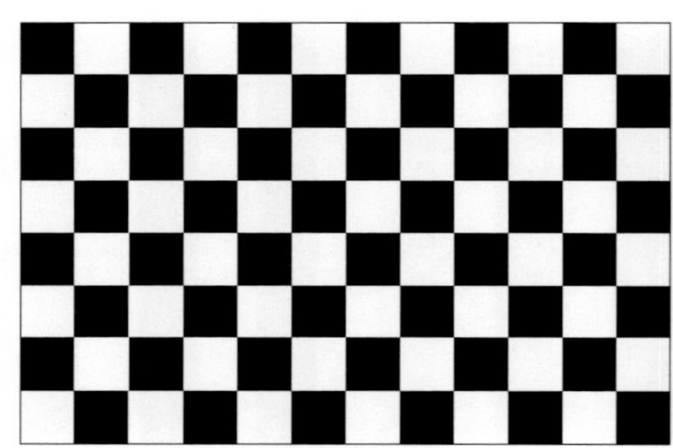

Brux chess
Jeroen Kramer

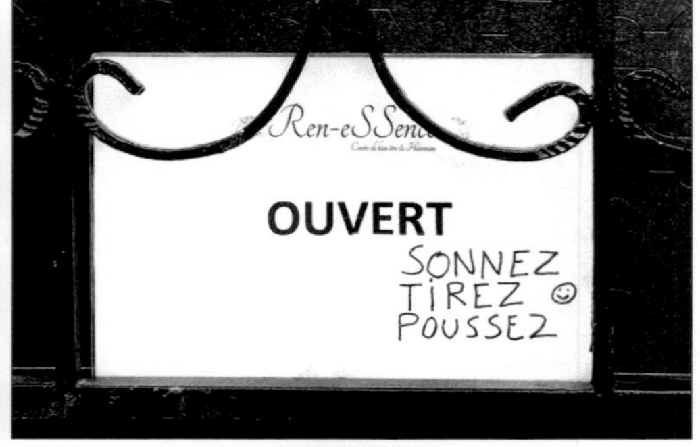

Open 24/7 BXL
Tina Lenz

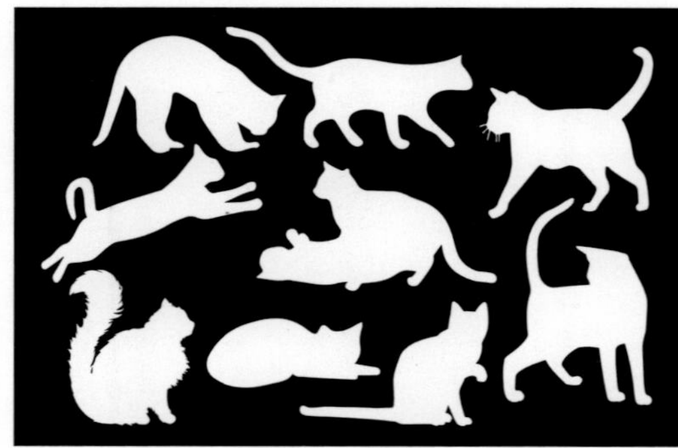

Catipal
Ellen Helsen

Flanders is Brussels is Wallonia
Caroline Dath *(Kidnap your designer)*

BeautyXL
Tina Lenz

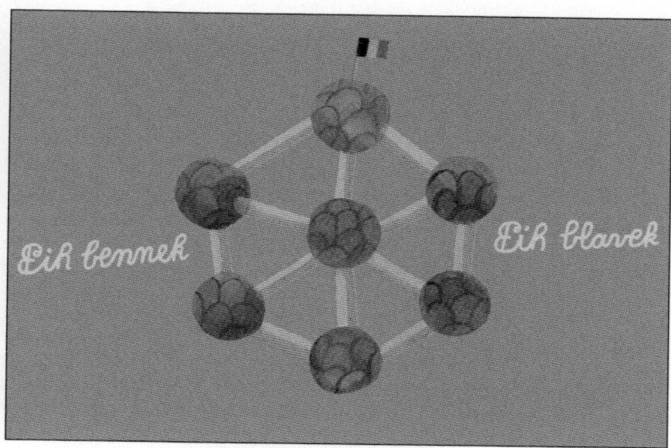

Eih bennek, eih blaivek
Tom Schamp

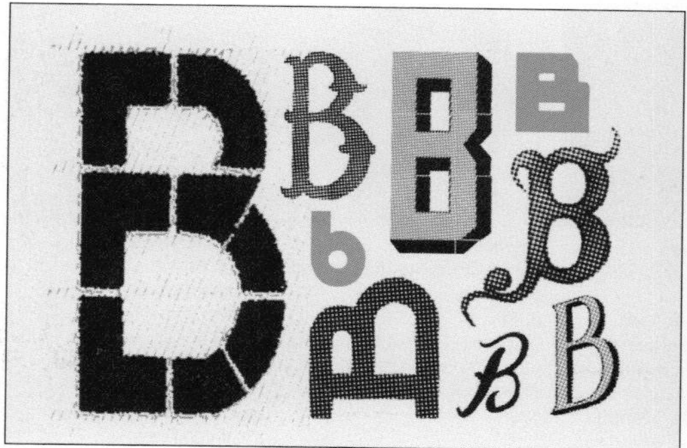

B-side
Vanessa Verbeiren

Bourraza thé
Amina Saâdi

Mix & match
Riitta Oittinen

Secret Passage
Shilezema Prins

INDEX OF CONTRIBUTORS

Amel Ben Ahmed
(2006, Ukkel, BE) Pupil
p. 14
Lives in Lot (Beersel) and goes to school in Anderlecht where she made a contribution for the *Subjective Atlas* as part of a workshop with artist Marianne Verwilghen.

Ilaria d'Auria
(1983, Rome, IT) Communication and project manager
p. 56
I met Brussels after eight other cities had broken my heart. I landed alone, and now have a second nationality, a home and a family. Brussels' imperfection makes our humanity more acceptable.

Joachim Ben Yakoub
(1982, Leuven, BE) PhD reseracher ***p. 114***
My father used to work in Brussels and I started working in the Pianofabriek in 2008 in Saint-Gilles, where the city and its inhabitants stole my heart. I moved to Molenbeek with my partner and to Sint-Agatha Berchem where we have become proud parents.

Dora Benyo
(1989, Budapest, HU) Visual artist
p. 58
I came three years ago to Brussels to do a master of arts and I have stayed ever since, as the city keeps interesting me.

Angélique Berhault *(1984, FR) Communication coordinator and graphic designer*
p. 94
I think that if Brussels were more green, people would be happy, joyful, and would care more for one another. They would always have subjects to talk about with their neighbours, such as the new flowers, plants and trees growing around.

Guido Bos
(1956, Hasselt, BE) Video cameraman
p. 21
Living in Brussels since 1978, at first for studies and later for work.

Vos Broekema
(1978, Amsterdam, NL) Designer and visual artist
p. 177
Brussels is like a country to me. I tend to listen to Studio Brussels on my car radio when I'm driving south for an instant holiday feeling. I remember wild nights after having worked late night shifts in Rotterdam's nightlife.

Elke Broothaers
(1986, Leuven, BE) Designer
p. 158
As I child I would visit Brussels with my parents for a restaurant or the Midi market. After a quiet life in the countryside, I longed for the hustle and bustle of the big city. I have lived here for 13 years and enjoy the city's many surprises.

Sophie Bruyr
(1991, Ottignies, BE) Interior architect / set designer
p. 15
I have been in love with the parks, bars and people of Brussels for the past seven years.

Etienne Buyse
(1953, Forest, BE) Administrator, freelance photographer
p. 152
I live, I love and I work in Brussels. It is for me a metropolis as well as a provincial town.

Pierre Cahurel
(1978, Saint-Nazaire, FR) Designer
p. 26, 28, 30, 32

Celine Callens
(1986, Kortrijk BE) Graphic designer, photographer
p. 130, 177
Living in Brussels for twelve years; I love the creativity of the city. It's a place where everybody can be themselves and express themselves.

Francesca Chiacchio
(1984, Milan, IT) Living drawing maker
p. 100
Living in Brussels for eight years now, I learned to wander around it and to observe it. This city is rich in contradictions and coincidences, where a week of sunshine quickly becomes a 'sun festival'.

Margrit Coppé
(1975, Leuven, BE) Graphic designer, publisher, author, teacher
p. 118
Born in Leuven, based in Brussels.

Frédéric Coppin
(1980, Leuven, BE) Recruiter
p. 15
Love brought me to Brussels in 2000. Ever since I have liked its human size and all it has to offer like culture, music and good food. Sometimes though, I would like it to be more dynamic, but I'm patient.

Almudena Crespo
(1957, Madrid, ES)
Visual artist
p. 86
I have lived and worked as an artist in Brussels since 1998.

Caroline Dath
(1983, Liège, BE)
Graphic designer
p. 176, 178
I came to study Graphic Design at ERG (École de Recherche Graphique) and I never left Brussels.
I set up a graphic design agency near Sainte-Catherine, more than ten years ago now.

Belinda De Bruyn
(1987, Leuven BE)
Graphic designer
p. 162
I studied at Sint-Lukas Brussels, but live in Berlin now.

Jorge de la Torre
(1964, México City, MX)
Visual artist
p. x176
A week after having my Master of Architecture in Mexico City, I flew to Brussels. Love brought and kept me. My twins were born in '01. I used to say when they're 18, I'll go. This time is close now, but I'm not sure that I want to leave.

Michael De Lausnay
(1972, Dendermonde, BE)
Photographer
p. 44
Pulled into the city while studying, and now settled in Molenbeek.

Mariska De Mey
(1964, Eeklo, NL) *Artist, mentor at Duo for a Job, branding specialist*
p. 120
I have lived in Brussels for 49 years and want to contribute to a greater mutual understanding between people from different cultures.

Johanna De Smet
(1996, Leuven, BE)
Student
p. 104
Lives in Brussels.

Annelys de Vet
(1974, Alkmaar, NL)
Initiator & editor of the Subjective Atlas of Brussels
p. 6, 170, 174
I moved to Brussels in 2007 out of love for the ungraspable quality and have lived for the past four years a stone's throw; in the Pajottenland, regularly bicycling to the centre.

Gilberte Debeer
(1951, BE) Retired and part-time art student at the Académie des beaux-arts de Bruxelles
p. 54
I love Brussels because of the lines, rhythms, patterns and graphics you can see everywhere in the infrastructure, like for example the zebra crossings.

Rob D'hondt
(1986, Sint-Niklaas, BE)
Environmental health officer at Doctors Without Borders
p. xx
Brussels has been my home base for my job abroad for the past six years. Each time I'm happy to come back because of the energy the city gives me and the beautiful view on the North district from the park at Tour & Taxis.

Rachelle Dufour
(1991, Lommel, BE)
Graphic designer, independent curator and cultural coordinator
p. 42
After my studies in Hasselt I moved to Brussels. For me the intense energy of the city flows like the soothing river Senne below us.

Sophie Feyder
(1983, Brussels, BE)
Researcher and story collector
p. 124, 176
I was born in Brussels, but didn't grow up here. Many years later, I chose this city as my home. I made the mapping of the places of hope to remind me why.

Lars Fisher
(1971, Duisburg, DE)
Architect
p. 66
In 2011 I moved from New York to Brussels.

Melat Gebeyaw Nigussie
(1991, Dessie, ET)
Writer, activist, project coordinator
p. 8
Brussels teaches me to see things anew, enriching me with unique perspectives each day as I roam its ever-changing streets.
It is the place I call home, the place that genuinely accepts me for who I am.

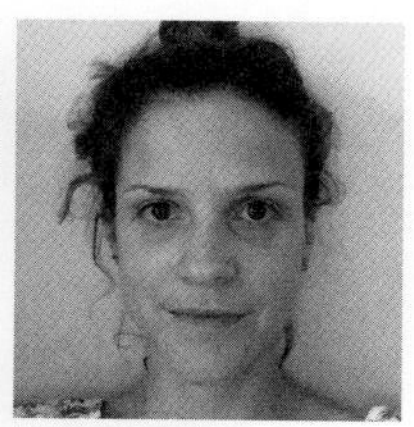

Mélanie Godin
(1980, Namur, BE)
Poetry entertainer
p. 34, 36
I live and work in Brussels with my family. It's a big city with the soul of a village.

Karel Goethals
(1981, Turnhout, BE)
Communication freelancer
p. 154
Although I have been living here a big part of my life, Brussels never bores me. I love to wander and wonder through its many backstreets without a fixed plan and stumble upon new things by chance.

Erik Gonzales
(1950, Santiago, CL) Artist at Globe Aroma, studied design at Universidad Catolica de Chile
p. 144
I like to show the emotions of the people in this city, I try to discover each personality by making portraits of them.

Hendrik Jan Grievink
(1977, Heerde, NL)
Designer
p. 177
Having visited Brussels just a few times, the city used to appear to me as a miniature version of Paris. Now, the word 'Brussels' has become an image that resonates with EU policymaking and bureaucracy.

Jessica Gysel *(1969, Bruges, BE) Editor & copywriter* ***p. 128***
Having lived in Amsterdam for over 16 years, I moved back to Brussels in 2014. Combining Dutch conceptual skills with Belgian laissez-faire, I nagivate the city much better than in the 90s. It has a lot to offer, but you need to dig deeper to fully grasp it. And persist!

Ellen Helsen
(1976, Schoten, BE)
Studied film in Brussels
p. 90, 178
I knew immediately that Brussels would be a long-term relationship; it's where my four kids were born, where you can be visible and invisible, travel without leaving and balance on the thin line between sweet forgivable absurdism and hard realism.

Miriam Hempel
(1979, Dachau, DE)
Designer
p. 98
After having lived in London for 11 years I found Brussels a hive of culture, diversity and quirkiness. One can keep travelling through different countries and atmospheres in Brussels and discover something new every time.

Elin Herlaar Masina
(2004, Elsene, BE) Student at the European School
p. 76
I was born and raised in Brussels and have lived here all my life. It is my home. Everywhere I walk I see memories, but I still manage to discover new places in it.

Christiane Högner
(1974, Tübingen, DE)
Designer
p. 172
Living and working in Brussels - sometimes admiring it, sometimes irritated by it.

Yazan Iwidat
(1991, Jerusalem, PS)
Dancer and marketer
p. 164
I moved to Brussels six years ago, to work as a dancer and then did my master's in marketing at ULB.

Céleste Joly
(1990, Paris, FR)
Illustrator
p. 70
I have lived in Brussels for the past four years and am studying illustration at La Cambre art school. I'm fascinated by the city's architecture, which is at once eclectic, fantastic and mysterious.

Catherine Jourdan
(1979, Amien, FR)
Psychoanalyst and artist
p. 26, 28, 30, 32

Omar Kashmiry
(1990, Cairo, EG)
Architect
p. 15, 18, 176, 178
Brussels as a cosmopolitan city is my second home. Its diversity gives me freedom and unlimited possibilities. A city that enriches one's journey and challenges the way we think.

Roel Kerkhofs
(1975, Brussel, BE) Artist, teacher of mixed media at LUCA School of Arts
p. 112
Born in Brussels, I also live and work here.

Maria Kley
(1981, Tokyo, JP)
Visual artist
p. 168
Brussels is hard to get, and therefore attractive. My challenge is to approach the city's chaos openly, without getting crazy, treasuring its richness. I came to Brussels for love. And my love is still there.

Jeroen Kramer
(1975, Schoorl, NL)
Artist, Head of designLAB, Gerrit Rietveld Academie
p. 178
Brussels is one of the true invisible cities where reality and fiction, surrealism and the unexpected are around every corner. Brussels is a state of mind and hard to get.

Germaine Kruip
(1970, Castricum, NL)
Artist
p. 102, 178
Having spent my childhood in Belgium, moving to Brussels from Amsterdam in 2009 allowed me to reconnect with my personal history while opening up new creative perspectives and relationships.

Tina Lenz
(1972, Alkmaar, NL)
Design anthropologist
p. 80, 178, 179
For ten years I walked through the labyrinth of Brussels as a *flâneur* surrounded by a crucible of cultures. It is the city that offered time and space to find my identity.

Eliana Liassides
(1966, CY) Graphic designer
p. 150
After five years in Brussels, I am still intrigued by its energy. My contribution aims to capture this energy through movement. Nothing in a city bonds people together in the way the metro does.

Rudy. J Luijters
(1955, The Hague, NL)
Artist
p. 96
In Brussels my life as an artist started 40 years ago. It became the center of my work, love and friends — and since 10 years it's my home base.

Khalil Masood
(1990, Gaza, PS) Photographer at Globe Aroma
p. 132, 134
I arrived two years ago in Belgium. I like the fact that there's always someting going on this city and the freedom is very big.

Abdel Doudou Medoki
(1981, TG) Fashion blogger and reporter, trendsetter
p. 146, 148
I moved to Brussels in 2006 from the Netherlands because I fell in love with this cosmopolitan city, dynamic and hospitality. The streets of Brussels have always inspired me and boosted my creativity.

Eveline Meijering
(1986, Wageningen, NL)
Design consultant
p. 84
Lives and works in Brussels.

Mia Melvær
(1988, Stavanger, NO)
Visual artist
p. 128
Brussels has kept me close to it for at least five years now. With its fragmented chaos and shape-shifting, it has become a fertile soil for a feminist and queer art scene on the rise.

Stijn Monsaert
(1982, Zottegem, BE)
Chemist
p. 19
I am fascinated by the city's plurality, multiculturality, alternative lifestyles and new developments. In Brussels I find my natural habitat.

Evelyne Morlot
(1989, Saint Germain-en-Laye, FR) Project manager at MAD Brussels
p. 166
I have lived for two years in Brussels with my Belgian boyfriend. The city is on a human scale and multicultural: walking distance everywhere. Colonial history can be found in flea markets and antique shops.

Riitta Oittinen
(1960, Helsinki, FI) Social historian, science journalist and urban activist
p. 60, 62, 64, 177, 179
I share my time between Brussels and Helsinki, and have been comparing their differences since 1995.

Nirit Peled
(1973, Rehovot, IL)
Film-maker
p. 140
Professional explorer turned part-time local. Hosted by sisters, the city became a place of retreat, recharging and conception.

Lucie Pinier
(1990, Angers, FR) Artist
p. 126, 177
...

Shilemeza Prins
(1962, Malmesbury, SA)
Artist at Globe Aroma
p. 110, 179
I've been a *Brusseleir* for twelve years. It is for me a very dynamic and empathic city where the old and the contemporary meet.

Adrien Requin
(1995, Avignon, Fr)
Graphic and type designer
p. 14
I moved here to start my quest on living a few years in cities around the world. I like the idea of having a home in several parts of the world and Brussels is my first new home.

INDEX OF CONTRIBUTORS

Amina Saâdi
(1991, Brussels, BE)
Graphic designer
p. 12, 13, 74, 176, 179
I'm born and raised in Brussels, and always enjoy to discover the different places and people. To me Brussels is a city or even not a city but something in between and it's what I like.

Saraa Saleh
(1975, Lattakia, SY)
Academic and artist
p. 138
Whenever I leave my house, the city places me in a confrontational position with myself and the world; we have been involved in a relationship for four years, in which both of us are constantly reformulating each other.

Tom Schamp
(1970, Mortsel, BE)
Illustrator
p. 22, 24, 179
I am an observing outsider with a historical and sometimes hysterical relation to my city. I lived for ten years in Jet-les-Bains and am increasingly keen to cycle through Brussels.

Erika Sprey
(1980, Leiden, NL)
Researcher and curator
p. 77
Moved from Amsterdam to Brussels in 2017 with my love Serge in search of inspiration. I love the city's layers, shadows and eclecticism, and hope to give birth to a new Ketje soon.

Funda Taşdan
(1984, Bergen op Zoom, NL)
Documentary film-maker
p. 160
As a regular visitor I'm intrigued and fascinated by the mixed colours of the city. I keep coming back to discover more.

Joud Toamah
(1992, Deir Azzor, SY)
Graphic designer
p. 92, 176
I visit Brussels from time to time and find it a challenging city. There is always something new to see and to learn which makes it fascinating.

Georgios Tziapouras
(1969, CY) *Political advisor, EU Parliament*
p. 156
The food we choose to eat is an expression for defining and affiliating ourselves with the community we live in. I celebrate Brussels multiculturalism by fusing harmoniously Brussels sprouts with various ethnic spices and delicacies.

Petra Van Brabandt
(1977,Ghent, BE) Philosopher working at arts college in Antwerp
p. 122
I moved from Flanders to Brussels twelve years ago and will never return. It was love at first, second and third sight.

Sofie Van Bruystegem
(1978, Leuven, BE) Urban micro-initiatives and prototyping at City Mine(d) since 2004
p. 106
Has lived and worked in and for Brussels since 2002.

Dorothé Van den Berghe
(1968, Ghent, BE)
Film-maker
p. 108
I moved to Brussels in 1990. For me it is the most inspiring place to create stories. It has been the setting for nearly all my films. The fractured character gives space for imagination, which is a treasure.

Filip Van Dingenen
(1975, Diest, BE) Artist
p. 41
Lives in and together with Brussels since 1999.

Judith Vanistendael
(1974, Leuven, BE) Author in words and drawings
p. 108
I grew up in the city since I was five years old and somehow I cannot get myself to leave this place. It is the water I learned to swim in, and as fish in the ocean, I even don't see the water anymore.

Lisemarie Van Loon
(1991, Merksem, BE)
Graphic designer & intern Subjective Atlas of Brussels
p. 136
What I like most about Brussels is the open mentality to different opinions: nobody is judging you, because we are all different and also the same. I always feel welcome.

Stephanie Vandergoten
(1986, Ninnove, BE)
Architect
p. 88
Something specific about this city is the special knobs at the doors, you cannot find this diversity in other countries. I came to Brussels and have now worked and lived here for the past three years.

Marjorie Vandriessche
(1989, Brussels, BE)
visit.brussels
p. 52
I arrived in Brussels to study 14 years ago. I've seen the city changing. Brussels is a fascinating puzzle, a constant work in progress. It's not always easy to find your place in it, you need to earn it. But once you have it, you're here forever.

Tarvo Varres
(1970, Tallinn, EE) Postconceptual artist, educator
p. 116
Exploring the nature of perception and decsion-making, one's sense of fluid identity and personal vertical time; I shot the work *Unavailable Memory* in Brussels over a month in 2014-15.

Vanessa Verbeiren
(1982, Brussels, BE)
Graphic designer
p. 78, 179
I was raised in Sint-Pieters-Woluwe, studied at Sint-Lukas Brussel and lived nine years in the Marolles. Brussels is the city I call 'home' even though I have lived for over a year in London now.

Anne Versailles
(1963, Brussels, BE)
Walker artist and geo-poet
p. 38, 39
I live in Brussels, in a small urban village surrounded by forest.

Laurence Vigin
(1974, Tournai, BE)
Geographer
p. 50
As I work in Brussels but live in another town, I use the train and bike to get to my work. Transport is an important factor for me, and biking in Brussels is always a challenge but also nice.

Pieterjan Volckaert
(1985, Ghent, BE)
Designer, visual storyteller
p. 142
Living in Brussels since 2009, I like to observe people from all backgrounds finding a place to hang out together. Beursplein (pedestrian area recently) is a hotspot for people to enjoy life away from car fumes and honking horns.

Alaa Zweid
(1979, Basrah, IQ)
Business assistant in a hotel
p. 20
I have lived in Brussels for the past three years. Brussels became my city and my home.

Visitors of MAD, during exhibition OCCUPATION: DESIGNER

An Vandermeulen, *p. 40*
Bastien, *p. 16*
G. P., *P. 15*
Hibo, *p. 14*
Ines Lionnez, *p. 14*
Nadim, *15*
Martha, *p. 16*
Mathi Deveau, *p. 16*
Romy & Mama, *p. 14*
Stefka, *p. 15*
Tanya, *p. 17*
Sandra, *p. 16*
Silvy, *p. 16*

MAPPING OF CONTRIBUTORS

Years of birth

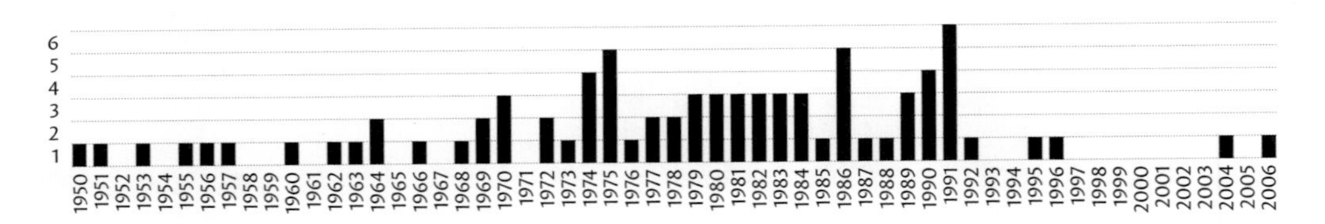

Countries of birth

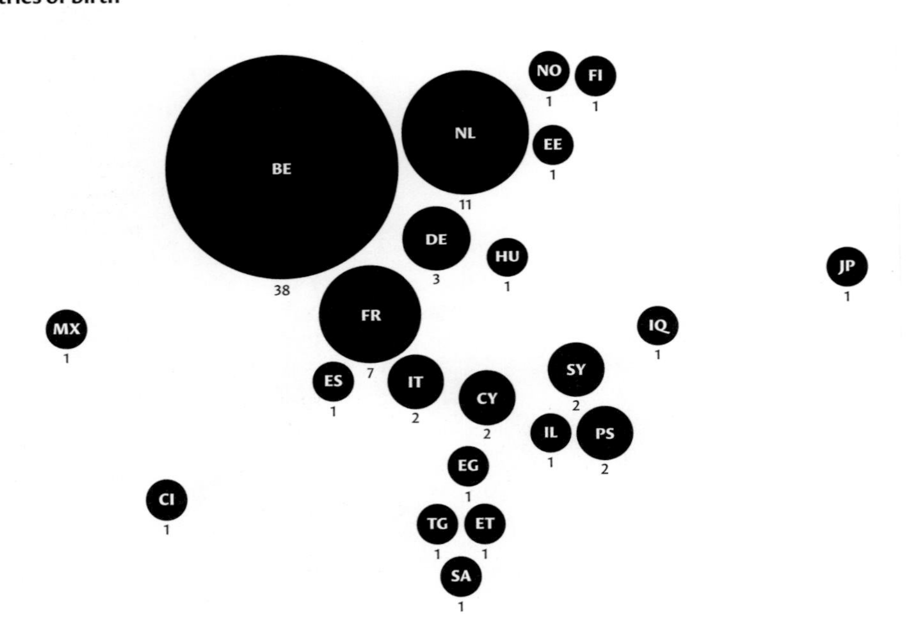

Gender

Country of birth

MAKING OF

The first contributions for the *Subjective Atlas of Brussels* were made as part of the exhibition OCCUPATION: DESIGNER at the fashion and design platform MAD Brussels. Visitors were invited to submit their works and MAD spread an open call to join several workshops by Annelys de Vet where the contributions were developed further. Among others, several artists who work at Globe Aroma joined these workshops. Based on this series, students from the Academy of Anderlecht were engaged by Margrit Coppé to also map Brussels from their personal perspective. Additionally a wide range of critical creatives were personally invited by the editors of this atlas to submit their subjective mappings of Brussels.

Lisemarie Van Loon

Workshop, MAD, 22 April 2017

Lisemarie Van Loon

Workshop, MAD, 23 April 2017

Lisemarie Van Loon

Workshop, MAD, 24 June 2017

Lisemarie Van Loon

Workshop, MAD, 27 July 2017

Margrit Coppé

Work discussion, Academie Anderlecht, 15 March 2018

Annelys de Vet

Work discussion, Academy of Anderlecht, 17 April 2018

Bottom-up cartographic publications mapping a country, region or city by the inhabitants themselves

Subjective Editions is a publishing initiative that develops and disseminates bottom-up engaged mapping publications. An expanding series of subjective atlases is being made in collaboration with local communities. These volumes map out a country, region or geopolitical entity in a personal way by the inhabitants themselves.

During workshops with local cultural institutes, artists, designers, photographers and architects are invited to map their country, environment, daily lives or social concerns from their own perspective. Personal involvement is the starting point to produce human, unconventional and fair images. The maps, graphs, inventories, flags and drawings as a whole expose the consequences of political change, but discreetly, implicitly, and not as a goal. The publications show, above all, a complex reality that is often blinded by overly simplistic media images.

This powerful series of alternative, copyright-free cartographies can serve as an inspiring, publicly available tool to critically question the apparently objective.

www.subjectiveatlas.info
www.facebook.com/subjectiveatlases

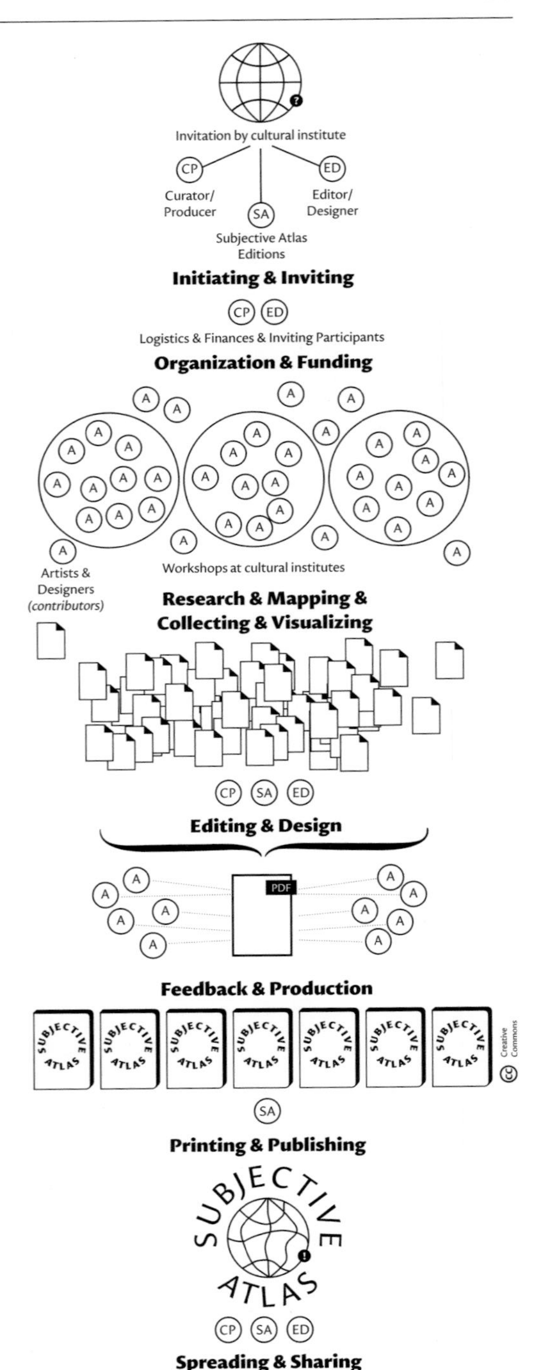

Subjectieve atlas van Nederland
(BIS Publishers, 2005) 128 p., Dutch.
Editor: Annelys de Vet. With Design Academy Eindhoven

Subjective atlas of Fryslân
(Afuk, 2013) 192 p, Dutch–Frysian–English.
Editor: Annelys de Vet. Curator: Roelof Koster.
With Keunstwurk, Academie voor Popcultuur

Subjective atlas of Serbia
(Dom Omladine, 2009) 128 p., English.
Editor: Annelys de Vet. Curator: Marija Kovac.
With Dom Omladine

Subjective atlas of Hungary
(HVG Könyvek & Kitchen Budapest, 2011) 192 p.,
English-Hungarian. Editor: Annelys de Vet.
Curator: Attila Bujdoso. With Kitchen Budapest

Subjective atlas of Hainaut
(Grand-Hornu Images, 2013) 192 p., French–English.
Editors/curators: Moniek Driesse, Annelys de Vet.
With Grand-Hornu Images, Féderation du Tourisme

Subjective atlas of Palestine
(010 Publishers, 2007) 160 p., English.
Editor: Annelys de Vet. Curator: Khaled Hourani.
With International Academy of Arts Palestine

Subjective atlas of Mexico
(LAST, 2011) 192 p., English-Spanish. Editors: Moniek Driesse, Annelys de Vet. Curators: Moniek Driesse, Analia Solomonoff. With Casa Vecina, Ule, Iago and Aavi

Subjective atlas of Colombia
(Semana Libros, 2015) 232 p., English-Spanish. Editors/curators: Moniek Driesse, Hugo Herrera Tobón, Annelys de Vet. With Universidad de los Andes, La Usurpadora

Subjective atlas of Pakistan
(Subjective atlas editions, 2018) 232 p., English.
Editors/curators: Taqi Shaheen, Annelys de Vet. With Department of Visual Studies, University of Karachi

COLOPHON

Editor-in-chief
Annelys de Vet

Research and editing
Petra van Brabandt, Margrit Coppé,
Lisemarie van Loon (intern), Erika Sprey

Introduction
Melat Gebeyaw Nigussie

Contributors
Amel Ben Ahmed, Ilaria d'Auria, Joachim Ben Yakoub, Dóra Benyó, Angélique Berhault, Guido Bos, Vos Broekema, Elke Broothaers, Sophie Bruyr, Etienne Buyse, Pierre Cahurel, Céline Callens, Francesca Chiacchio, Margrit Coppé, Frédéric Coppin, Almudena Crespo, Caroline Dath, Belinda De Bruyn, Jorge de la Torre, Michael De Lausnay, Mariska De Mey, Johanna De Smet, Annelys de Vet, Gilberte Debeer, Mathi Deveau, Rob D'hondt, Rachelle Dufour, Sophie Feyder, Lars Fischer, Mélanie Godin, Karel Goethals, Erik Gonzalez, Hendrik Jan Grievink, Jessica Gysel, Ellen Helsen, Miriam Hempel, Elin Herlaar Masina, Christiane Högner, Yazan Iwidat, Céleste Joly, Catherine Jourdan, Omar Kashmiry, Roel Kerkhofs, Maria Kley, Jeroen Kramer, Germaine Kruip, Tina Lenz, Eliana Liassides, Ines Lionnez, Rudy J. Luijters, Abdel Doudou Medoki, Eveline Meijering, Mia Melvær, Stijn Monsaert, Evelyne Morlot, Riitta Oittinen, Khalil Masood, Nirit Peled, Lucie Pinier, Shilemeza Prins, Adrien Requin, Amina Saâdi, Saraa Saleh, Tom Schamp, Erika Sprey, Funda Taşdan, Joud Toamah, Georgios Tziapouras, Petra Van Brabandt, Sofie Van Bruystegem, Dorothée Van den Berghe, Filip Van Dingenen, Judith van Istendael, Lisemarie van Loon, Stephanie Van der Goten, Marjorie Vandriessche, Tarvo Varres, Vanessa Verbeiren, Anne Versailles, Laurence Vigin, Pieterjan Volckaert, Alaa Zweid

Graphic design
Annelys de Vet in collaboration
with all the contributors

Proofreading
Patrick Lennon

Cover image
Saraa Saleh

Typeface
Proza by Jasper de Waard

Acknowledgements
MAD Brussels, Academie Anderlecht, Globe Aroma (Els Rochette, Liselore van der Put), Beursschouwburg Brussel, Tunde Adefioye, Riitta Otten and all those who were involved; without your beneficent, inspiring and critical support this book wouldn't have been possible.

With the generous support of

Printer
Artoos Group

Publisher
Subjective Editions
(Annelys de Vet, Kurt Vanbelleghem)

Contact
www.subjectiveatlas.info
info@subjectiveatlas.info

ISBN
978-9-08-291990-5